FREELANCE IN FRANCE

I0390657

2015

BARTH HULLEY

Cover image by NH! © 2010

© B Hulley, Strasbourg, 2015
ISBN 978-1-326-15300-7

Contents

Foreword

When I moved to France in 2006 there was almost no advice or support for people who wanted to work as freelancers in *La République*. There seemed to be books aplenty for people wanting to convert a barn into a *gite*, run a ski chalet or retire to the Dordogne; but nothing, *rien*, for those of us who simply wanted to earn a living in our new home away from home.

Upon arrival in France I was not short of information, though it was often of little use because almost no-one I met had actually had any first-hand experience of being self-employed themselves. Which meant most of the advice I received was either ill-informed or just plain wrong. Trial and error seemed to be the only way forward and I made my fair share of errors, which ultimately resulted in the demise of my first freelance business in France.

Thankfully things have changed for the better since then. All the information you need is now freely available online and it's possible to complete many of the formalities, that were once only possible with a pen in hand, electronically. In 2009 the Sarkozy government introduced a new, fairer, statute for independents called the *auto-entrepreneur*, for which the net result was the creation of thousands of new businesses overnight. The growing success of the *portage salarial* and *cheque emploi* schemes have also made life easier, however, things are still far from simple. With earning limits, several legal structures and numerous *charges* to account for, understanding your obligations can still be very difficult. Furthermore, since the sovereign debt crisis hit in 2010, government legislators have been tinkering with the rules concerning many freelance statutes in order to save money.

Today there are sixteen recognised ways to work for yourself in France, but you need to know the difference between each option, what you're allowed to do, what you're not allowed to do, what you're required to do and the pros and cons of each before you can make an informed decision. Hopefully you'll find all the information you need to get you started right here.

If I'd had this book back in 2006, along with the new choice of statutes, I would most certainly have become a millionaire by now.

Introduction

First let's get a few things straight. This guidebook is intended purely as a starting point to help you get set up as an independent worker in France. That is, it's designed to help you understand the fundamental rules and regulations that govern the way you do business as a freelancer in *la République,* the choices available to you and where to go for more information. Also, because you are probably already aware of, and feel somewhat nervous about, the nation's reputation for bureaucracy –it is also aimed at helping you overcome any fears you might have about the French system and give you the confidence to get going.

Note though that this book is aimed at readers who already have a good understanding of business, but simply need some guidance as to how to get up and running in France. So if you've never worked for yourself before and are looking for some advice on how to do business in general then you need to look elsewhere. There are plenty of good books out there that will give you reams of excellent advice on the ins and outs of supply chain management, good customer service, strategic pricing, staying motivated, etcetera... but this isn't one of them.

Equally, if you are looking for specialist advice on the tax implications of working in France then, again, you've come to the wrong place. While you will find information on general tax arrangements and social charges within these pages, I have not covered them in any significant detail. International tax law is such a monumental beast that it would require several more books to explain –per year. If you need help you should seek the advice of an accountant with up-to-date knowledge of both France and your home country's taxation systems.

So if you know your margin from your PBIT and your turnover from your cost-base, then please keep reading.

The first thing you need to appreciate is the French attitude towards free enterprise; in general, they are suspicious of anyone who wishes to go it alone. This is because, historically, starting your own business in France was often seen as a lengthy and somewhat costly process. Meaning independent wealth was usually required beforehand in order to ensure success. If you were prepared to go it alone therefore, that obviously meant you had buckets of cash stowed away somewhere, most likely illicitly. This suspicion manifests itself today as a total absence of incentives and rewards for your efforts. That is, there is nothing to attract you away from a safe salaried nine-to-five in the name of free enterprise, other than the possibility of becoming your own boss.

Indeed, as a freelancer, you usually pay a greater proportion of what you earn into state coffers than as an employee. Then, if you become successful, you are liable to pay even more again. This is because the French regard retirement with a well-funded pension pot as the ultimate reward for working hard. The more you earn – the better your pension will be. What more could you possibly want? Freelancing therefore is often seen as the ideal second job.

Taxation in France

Despite what you might hear income tax rates in France, *les impôts*, are not actually that high in comparison to other Western nations. While the base-rates of tax might seem steep, in practice, if you are married and have children, you will actually pay significantly less.

Every household, or *foyer*, in France is required to file a tax return each year. The tax year is identical to the calendar year, running January to December, with returns usually filed in May. Usually, you are informed of how much tax you owe for the previous year in September and are expected to settle any arrears before Christmas. If you have anything to pay you are encouraged to set up a monthly direct debit so that you can start paying your tax bill for the following year from January (even though you, nor the state, know how much you actually owe yet!) The tables below show an example of how your income is taxed according to your household status.

Individual (unmarried without children)		Family (married with 3 children)	
Income 2014	Tax rate	Income 2014	Tax rate
Up to 9,690 €	0 %	Up to 19,380 €	0 %
9,690 to 26,764 €	14 %	19,380 to 53,528 €	14 %
26,764 to 71,754 €	30 %	53,528 to 143,508 €	30 %
71,754 to 151,956 €	41 %	143,508 to 303,912 €	41 %
More than 151,956 €	45 %	More than 303,912 €	45 %

For example: an individual earning 50,000€ would pay about 19% income tax, whereas a family with 3 children earning the same amount would pay only 3%. If you want to find out how much you will have to pay for your particular situation there's a handy calculator on Le Figaro's website: lefigaro.fr/simulation-impot-sur-le-revenu/

All households in France (tax resident or not) are also required to pay a residency tax known as the *Taxe d'habitation*. This usually also includes your audio-visual (TV) license and is normally billed in November. It is means tested and calculated according to the value of the property you live in. Again, you are encouraged to pay in advance by direct debit.

Pensions, Health, Social Security...

This is where things get expensive. If you take a look at the average French payslip you will see a long list of deductions covering a whole range of compulsory payments for: health, unemployment, pension, professional training, insurance, social taxes, debt relief, family allowance, old-age solidarity, etc. which together are known as *les charges patronales*. Ironically, because they usually appear as an incomprehensible list of acronyms (which will vary according to your trade, role and location), the majority of French people have little idea what most of the lines on their payslip really mean, nor where their money actually goes after it is deducted. These *charges* should not account for more that 30% of gross pay unless you have decided to take out complementary health insurance (known as *le mutuel* or *complementaire*) or additional pension cover, in which case deductions might exceed 35% before tax.

This is not where the pain ends for the freelancer however. There are additional deductions called *les charges salariales* which are settled by your employer but do not appear on your payslip. These account for another 20% or so of your *masse salariale* (total

11

wage as allocated by your employer). Now, why should you care what your employer pays on top of your own pay-packet? Well, if you are a freelancer, the state may consider you, depending upon your 'statute', as your own employer (i.e. you employ yourself as well as work for yourself) –and therefore you will be expected to settle both the *patronale* and *salariale* charges at the same time; meaning total deductions could exceed 45%.

If you thought things were complicated enough to understand already they are made positively opaque by the variation in payments according to how much you earn. As with income tax, the amount deducted from your wage for any given fund or policy will vary according to your income band, household status and professional qualifications.

All this means it is almost impossible to give any categorical answer to the question "So how much do I have to pay?" Anecdotal indications, like those you will find here, can be your only guide. In most instances it is likely you will only know how much you have to pay –after you've paid it!

Below is a breakdown from a real *CESU déclaratif* payroll slip, in both French and English, for you to compare.

MONTANT DÉTAILLÉ DES COTISATIONS SOCIALES						
Détail des cotisations	Cotisations Salariales			Cotisations Patronales		
CSG + CRDS	153,33 x	2,900% =	4,45			
CSG DEDUCTIBLE	153,33 x	5,100% =	7,82			
MALADIE	156,06 x	2,250% =	3,51	156,06 x	12,800% =	19,98
VIEILLESSE	156,06 x	7,150% =	11,16	156,06 x	10,300% =	16,08
ALLOC. FAMILIALES				156,06 x	5,250% =	8,19
ACCIDENT DU TRAVAIL				156,06 x	2,200% =	3,43
FNAL				156,06 x	0,100% =	0,16
CFP				156,06 x	0,250% =	0,39
CSA				156,06 x	0,300% =	0,47
COS				156,06 x	0,016% =	0,02
IRCEM	156,06 x	3,870% =	6,04	156,06 x	3,880% =	6,06
IRCEM PREVOYANCE	156,06 x	0,700% =	1,09	156,06 x	0,910% =	1,42
AGFF	156,06 x	0,800% =	1,25	156,06 x	1,200% =	1,87
POLE EMPLOI	156,06 x	2,400% =	3,75	156,06 x	4,000% =	6,24
Total :			39,07 €			64,31 €

DETAILS OF SOCIAL CHARGES						
Details	Employer Contributions			Employee Contributions		
SOCIAL SECURITY + SOCIAL DEBT	153,33 x	2,900% =	4,45			
DEDUCTIBLE SOCIAL SECURITY	153,33 x	5,100% =	7,82			
SICKNESS (HEALTH)	156,06 x	2,250% =	3,51	156,06 x	12,800% =	19,98
OLD AGE (PENSION)	156,06 x	7,150% =	11,16	156,06 x	10,300% =	16,08
FAMILY ALLOWANCE				156,06 x	5,250% =	8,19
WORKPLACE ACCIDENT				156,06 x	2,200% =	3,43
HOUSING BENEFIT				156,06 x	0,100% =	0,16
PROFESSIONAL TRAINING				156,06 x	0,250% =	0,39
SOLIDARITY FOR THE INFIRM/HANDICAPPED				156,06 x	0,300% =	0,47
UNION SERVICES				156,06 x	0,016% =	0,02
RETIREMENT	156,06 x	3,870% =	6,04	156,06 x	3,880% =	6,06
INSURANCE	156,06 x	0,700% =	1,09	156,06 x	0,910% =	1,42
EARLY RETIREMENT	156,06 x	0,800% =	1,25	156,06 x	1,200% =	1,87
POLE EMPLOI (UNEMPLOYMENT)	156,06 x	2,400% =	3,75	156,06 x	4,000% =	6,24
Total :			39,07 €			64,31 €

After deductions, the employee was paid a net total of 117€ from a total wage packet of 220.38€ for 9 hours' work. The employer's contributions accounting for 39.07€ and the employee's for 64.31€. The employee will have no visibility of the charges settled by the employer as these do not appear on their payslip. While gross pay is 181.31€ (net pay 117€ + employee contributions

64.31€) calculations for social charges are actually based upon net pay plus the <u>employer's</u> contributions (117€ + 39.07€ = 156.06€[1]).

Note that the amount of income that the employee declares on their annual tax return will be their net wage plus the non-deductible social security payment paid by the employer; in this case: 117€ + 4.45€ = 121.45€.

You may also have to settle what are known as *regularisations* of your charges. These are usually only applicable to people whose income varies from month to month (i.e. freelancers) and they compensate for any possible underfunding of a *caisse* (fund) due to low income. You might, for example, earn nothing in May but then thousands in June – however your June *charges* will include payment for the funds you were unable to pay into in May.

Benefits and training

Given that you pay out so much to the Republic you should feel no shame in claiming your dues back from the state whenever you can.

In addition to standard social security benefits like Family Allowance (*Allocation Familiale*) and job-seekers allowance

---

[1] I know, it should be 156.07€ right?

(ASSEDIC), if your income is deemed low for your household, you may often be entitled to claim childcare allowance (CmG), back-to-school benefit (ARS), single parent benefit (ASF), baby/toddler-care allowance (CLCA), sickness/disabled care allowances, income support (RSA) or housing benefit (*Aide Logement*). Again, as with income tax, if you are married with children you are more likely to qualify for support than if you are living alone. Most benefits are also subject to means testing. Note however, you cannot apply for the majority of benefits until you have been tax resident in France for at least 9 months.

You can apply for income support (RSA) if your income remains low for three consecutive months. If you qualify for support, payments will begin the following month (i.e. 4-5 months after your business collapsed!) with reviews of your situation every subsequent quarter. Housing benefit is usually calculated in November and paid per month from January to December. It is reviewed annually.

If you have already worked in France and are claiming benefits, you can also take advantage of a welfare-to-work scheme known as ACCRE which offers discounts on social contributions under a number of freelance structures.

The *Caisse d'Allocations Familiales (CAF)* publish an English language guide to help foreigners get to grips with the ins and outs of the French Benefits system. Visit www.caf.fr/international for more information.

If you are an employee or self-employed in France you are also entitled to professional training every year. The number of hours and the type of training you are entitled to will depend upon your professional status and the number of hours worked. The first step is to create an account at moncompteformation.gouv.fr where you will find all the options available to you.

Fraternity

It is perhaps worth pointing out that cash benefits and training are not all you get back from the French government. Much of France's state coffers go into community, regional and national projects that are designed to benefit the public as a whole. While less tangible than cash, this is where the real benefit of French living resides.

In case you were wondering, socialist philosophy still lies at the heart of French politics. The reason for this goes right back to the French revolution, the 'Declaration of the Rights of Man and of the Citizen' and the subsequent adoption of the nation's *devise* (slogan): *Liberté, Égalité, Fraternité* (Freedom, Equality, Fraternity); these principles underscore the foundations of *La Republique* even today.

While freedom and equality are by no means the exclusive domain of the French, few western nations embrace the principle of fraternity (brotherhood) to the same extent; and it is this that gives France its pseudo-socialist reputation. Even the National Front (FN), one of France's more right-wing political parties, takes a largely socialist stance towards care of the populous.

Socialism, in its very broadest sense, is based upon the belief that every member of a community shares the responsibility for the well-being of every other member of that community. In practice, and according to interpretation, this means that each individual in a community contributes a proportion of their resources, as taxes, for the good of the community. How much is contributed and what constitutes 'the good of the community' varies wildly according to the political standpoint.

Capitalism is often presented as being incompatible with socialism; however, this is not true. It is possible to make capital while providing for your fellow man and community, but the extent to which this provision is made will depend on political will and the support of the electorate. In the USA they find it hard to justify expenditure on universal healthcare for example while elsewhere this would be seen as a basic right of every citizen.

In France, there is a widespread belief that the delivery of good public services is the primary purpose and responsibility of elected representatives –over and above a thriving economy even. In Britain the inverse is probably true with public services progressively deconstructed in the belief that it saves money for the public purse while providing opportunity for private enterprise to flourish.

The problem in societies where public services are run by the private sector is that profits are often placed before the public good, not least because a company that does not make a profit will not survive. Companies that run any kind of public service therefore are likely to compromise on quality in order to secure higher margins.

Opponents of a high-tax society argue that it's not possible to guarantee high quality public services as there is no element of competition in their provision, therefore there is no impetus to improve either the efficiency or the quality of service. While this seems a logical assumption it is hard to ignore how the French have managed to do just that.

France has one of the highest percentages of government expenditure to GDP in the world –meaning its taxpayers have a tax burden to match. However, affordable public transport, first-class healthcare, free childcare from age 3, free schools and universities, Europe's fastest rail network, modern leisure and sports facilities, theatres, museums, concert halls, libraries, protected forests, mountains, vineyards... everything, in fact, that you might expect to get from paying your taxes, suggest it may be a price worth paying.

Language

It would be wrong to insist that you need a good level of French before starting your own business in the Republic; however, it would be equally wrong to suggest that you could remain blissfully ignorant of the language forever.

Despite the increasing accuracy of translation apps and the growing availability of online account filing, chances are you'll have to deal with face-to-face communication at some point, and that's when your grasp of French will get found out. Hiring an English-speaking accountant or asking a bilingual friend to see you through are possible solutions, albeit temporary ones. However, it is your duty as a resident of France to learn French, not least in order to follow the changes in legislation that affect your business.

Learning to speak French is not something you should regard as a finite project either. While it may only take a few months to pick up the essentials, it will take you years to perfect. Indeed, you will probably have retired by the time you feel you have nothing left to learn.

This might seem daunting, especially if you feel you don't have the knack for languages. Certainly, when I learned French at school, I never felt I could communicate using it. I put this down to my inability to regurgitate information and a lack of vocabulary in the language. However, the real reason for my incapacity became clear after I completed audio course taught by Frenchman *Michel Thomas*, some twenty years later. Thomas's method is based around what he calls 'internalisation', where there's no need for homework, reading or writing; you just sit back and soak it up. While this might sound too good to be true, I found the reality was quite the contrary. In a very short space of time I learned that the key to unlocking a language was neither the vocabulary, pronunciation nor the ability to memorise a book-full of phrases, it was quite simply —the grammar. A clear, if basic, understanding of French grammar enabled me to start communicating coherently in a very short space of time. Fluency, and the ability to sound remotely intelligent, took significantly longer though.

Like all languages, French is inextricably linked to French culture and society, so you also need to take an interest in France's history, arts and traditions too. This will help you to enrich your vocabulary with the household names and cultural references that are common knowledge across France, as well as help you understand far more of what's going on around you. For example, if you can't identify names such as *Giscard d'Estaing, Plantu, Cauet, Les Enfoirés, Maître Gims or Jean-Pierre Foucault*, you're going to find conversation (and therefore business) in France a bit of a trial.

Getting your Carte Vitale

Without a doubt your first objective, once you've set up your freelance business, should be to acquire your *carte vitale*. This little, green, credit-card sized piece of plastic, that bears your social security number will make your life a lot simpler. Over and above its uses as proof of health cover it is also the key that links your pension, social security and other *patronale* contributions together.

Without it, you will have to provide alternative proof of identity to the many *caisses* (funds) that you'll have to deal with (usually in the form of reams of photocopies of official documents accompanied by letters that attest to your identity, background and status etcetera) so once you've got it, chances are you'll have significantly less paperwork to do.

Assurance Maladie, the French Health Insurance body, offer information in English on their website www.ameli.fr as well as English speaking advice on 08.11.36.36.46 from Monday to Friday 9 am to 6 pm.

Financing your activity

Business in France is made particularly difficult by the rules regarding debt. In theory, you are not allowed to get into debt at all. Although there is a certain degree of flexibility, at the end of every month your bank account must hold money in it. Any lack of funds will result in a "helpful" call from your branch manager asking you to find some money to put into your account –pronto. Writing a cheque when you have no money is considered a felony; indeed, if one of your cheques bounces and you do not settle the payment by other means within 30 days you could quickly find yourself barred from holding a bank account and facing a 5 year jail term and/or a six figure fine.

Loans, credit cards and overdrafts do exist in France, however they are far from being the fair, flexible financial facilities they are in the UK and the US. You are usually required to provide evidence of guarantee or be earning at least three times the sum requested.

The Euro

It is natural that you may have some reservations about doing business in the Eurozone, following the widely publicised sovereign debt crises in Greece, Spain and Ireland. Indeed, it seems some economists are nothing short of enthusiastic in predicting the Euro's demise. However, it's worth bearing in mind just how strong the currency really is and how vital a role it plays within the EU.

Today there are approximately one trillion Euros in circulation, in the form of banknotes and coins, making it the world's largest currency, ahead of the US Dollar even. It is used daily by over 300 million people across the continent to buy anything from a loaf of bread to an Airbus A380. This makes it incredibly stable and shields it from manipulation by currency speculators. Also, at the time of writing, the Eurozone was enjoying its highest ever trade surplus, meaning companies around the world are happier than ever to do business with it.

In 2011, at the height of the supposed crisis, a report by the Economist Intelligence Unit summed up the Eurozone's strengths:

"[...] if the region is treated as a single entity, its position looks no worse and in some respects, rather better than that of the US or the UK. In 2010 the budget deficit for the euro area as a whole is estimated at 6.2% of GDP admittedly high, but much lower than the budget deficit posted by the US (an estimated 8.9% of GDP) and the UK (10.1% of GDP). The euro area's government debt/GDP ratio was around 86% about the same level as the US. Moreover, private-sector indebtedness across the euro area as a whole is markedly lower than in the highly leveraged Anglo-Saxon economies."

The problem, it seems, is not an economic one. It is the fact that the Euro is not controlled by a single nation state that worries the money men. The politics of the Euro are unlikely to be ironed-out overnight, however.

As a freelancer in France the only thing that should concern you is the exchange rate, should you be doing business with clients outside the Eurozone. You have to remember that because you will be declaring and paying all your social security and taxes in Euros, in some cases on a monthly basis, you'll need to be able to predict just how much will be arriving in your bank account from month to month. It is safest, and simplest therefore, to always bill your clients in Euros wherever they are and whenever possible.

Freelance Options

Although there are only five legal freelance structures to choose from in France (auto-entrepreneur, EI Regime Classique, EIRL, EURL and SASU), in practice there are many ways to work for yourself, be it within the confines of a one of these structures or otherwise. In the following section I detail each option relevant to individuals wishing to pursue a genuine freelance activity; having excluded anything that requires a second person to set up; because the moment that happens things get a lot more complicated!

So which option should you choose? Well, that will depend upon a number of factors – not least the type of work you're going to be doing.

1. 90 day rule
2. Au noir
3. Travailleur frontalier
4. Fille au pair
5. Chèques emploi (CESU)
6. Auto entrepreneur
7. Travailleur Indépendant
8. Artiste-Auteur
9. Intermittent de spectacle
10. Portage Salarial
11. CAE
12. EIRL/AERL
13. EURL
14. SASU
15. SELARL/SELAS

As a general rule, if you are going to be turning over less than 30,000€ a year you should opt for the *auto entrepreneur* statute as this ensures you only pay 23%

of your revenue to the authorities and you will not be embroiled in the paperwork and regulations that accompany many of the other legal statuses. If you are a creative person or have anything to do with the creative arts then you should consider the *intermittent du spectacle* and *EI Artiste-Auteur* statuses which also offer preferential social security rates. Equally, for those just starting out, choosing a CAE could be an attractive option. If you are providing unskilled personal services then the *CESU declaratif* system is probably the best place to start. Unless you are a qualified practitioner of a regulated trade, then you should consider *Portage Salarial* if you want to charge VAT and provide professional services or advice.

The remaining statutes (Travailleur Indépendant, EURL, SASU and SELARL/SELAS) represent a step change in terms of complexity and therefore should only be considered by those whose predicted future turnover is likely to be significant and – more importantly –steady. Peaks and troughs in your year-to-year sales figures will cause no end of headaches!

1.   The 90 day rule

Can't you just avoid all the stress by saying you're just in France on an extended holiday? Well yes, but not for long. You are not required to declare yourself resident in France until after 90 days. This period equates to the maximum holiday time you are allowed to spend, continuously, in the country without being considered permanent.

In theory this means you have approximately three months to try out life in France before committing. However, finding property to rent for just three months can be difficult and expensive. So you may decide it's just simpler to commit from the outset and just roll with it.

Professionally speaking, if you are a freelancer in your country of origin, this means you can continue your trade in France for 3 months without having to make any formal declaration of your whereabouts. Beyond the 90 days you will have to make a decision one way or the other.

2.   Au noir

Translation Moonlighting / black market

Description Cash only.

Pros No paperwork. No taxes.

Cons Illegal. Risk of imprisonment (3 years) and a fine of
45,000 €. Loss of benefits.
No health or social cover.

Practised by Illegal immigrants, children, drug dealers, arms dealers,
evil geniuses, gung-ho tradesmen frustrated by French
protectionist practices and just about anyone employed
by someone carrying a suitcase full of cash.

I landed on French shores with the assumption that doing business above-board was the rule not the exception –when the inverse was probably true.

Cash-in-hand or *travail au noir* appears to be the more accepted first step on the rung of self-employment in France. Although it is, in the strictest terms, illegal –there is little the authorities can do to clamp down on transactions between individuals; so it goes on *sans cesse*. They say that you can tell when someone's been working *au noir* because their wallet will be full of 100 € notes.

It isn't hard to see why *au noir* is considered an acceptable way of doing business in France. Anyone buying a house or an apartment is often asked to make a cash payment as part of the completion process in order to lower the recorded sale value. A lower sale value means less capital gains tax for the seller. This practice is illegal but it happens regularly.

In recent times two former Presidents, Sarkozy and Chirac, have been caught up in scandals attributed to their predilection for handling brown envelopes stuffed with cash. No wonder then, certainly if the country's leaders are at it, why the populous regard tax-evasion as such a minor misdemeanour.

I am not recommending you do it, though it is worth noting that some people consider it a viable option; a view held not exclusively by people in France of course!

Au noir

3. Travailleur frontalier

Translation	Border worker
Description	Live in France, freelance abroad.
Pros	Higher earnings. Real croissants for breakfast. Two year grace period for EU/EEA citizens.
Cons	Short-term solution. Tax and social security arrangements are subject to all sorts of complex and constantly changing legislation.
Suitable for	Self-employed EU/EEA citizens spending less than two years in France. Anyone with a client-base entirely outside of France.
Tax	Unless you spend less than 183 days in France per year, you must let the authorities know that you are a tax resident in France. It is best to contact the Welcome Centre for Non-Residents (SANR) for advice and an official view of your tax obligations.

Accounts	You may need an astute accountant and/or lawyer to help keep you on the right side of the law.

Health, Pension and Social Security contributions	If you are an EU/EEA citizen you can work in France and remain covered by your home-country social security system for up to two years. If you wish to do this, you need to apply for a European A1 form (formerly the E 101 form) which proves that you and your dependants are still covered by your home system while in France.

To be eligible, you have to prove that the activities you intend to pursue in France are similar to, or the same as, those you pursued in your home country.

You can only remain covered by your home system for two years. To benefit from French healthcare during this period you must carry a European Health Insurance Card (formerly the E111 form). After that you have to switch to the French system.

Non EU/EEA citizens need to take out private healthcare cover or risk substantial hospital bills.

If you are self-employed in your home country and non-tax resident in France, and not covered by the

EU/EEA 2-year agreement, you are required to pay compulsory social security contributions using URSSAF's *Titre particulier employeur étranger* (TPEE) or Titre firmes étrangères (TFE) online payment systems and, where necessary, register yourself as a foreign employer with the CNFE. (see www.tpee.urssaf.fr, www.tfe.urssaf.fr and www.anglais.urssaf.fr for more information). These contributions will amount to around 40% of real gross wage.

Getting started You need to already be set up as a freelance worker in your country of origin.

If you're concerned about your tax obligations, a welcome centre for non-residents and expatriates (SANR), with English speaking support, is available to assist anyone planning to move to France.

The role of this special advice centre is to provide legal and tax advice appropriate to your situation, by determining how French and European tax rules apply to you. As an initial step you can book an individual appointment to ask for information or a simulation of your theoretical tax obligations.

As soon as you've taken the decision to establish your tax residence in France, you can ask SANR to adopt a formal position in the form of an *advanced tax ruling*. If you wish to use this option you have to write a formal letter of request to SANR, accompanied by supporting documents. This is recommended if your situation is particularly complicated or unusual.

The offices of SANR are located in Paris:

Direction Générale des Finances Publiques

Service d'accueil des non-résidents et expatriés (SANR)

Bureau des agréments et rescrits - Service juridique de la fiscalité

86-92 allée de Bercy

Télédoc 957

75574 PARIS Cedex 12

T: +33 (0)1.53.18.19.46

E: sanr@dgfip.finances.gouv.fr

4.   Fille au pair

Description   Live-in child carer

Pros   Live with real French people. Learn French. All meals
                  and accommodation included.

Cons   You usually have to live with your employer.
                  Payment in kind *(nature)* only. If your employer pays
                  you a wage then you are no longer considered an *Au*
                  pair.

Suitable for   Anyone aged 18-29 years.

Wages   None, however perks can include a discretionary
                   "pocket money" allowance, local transport costs and
                   French lessons.

Accounts   Easy, once you've signed an employment contract,
                      you don't have to do a thing. Your employer is
                      required to file all of your details with URSSAF.

Health, Pension and Social Security contributions	Your employer pays these based on the value of your *nature* (food and board). This covers you for pension, social security, health and training. Meals are currently valued at 4.70€ each and lodging at 71€ per month – meaning your effective net wage will be viewed as equivalent to 500€ per month.
Other formalities	All agencies charge various fees for taking you on as well as finding you a placement. Contracts range from 2 months to 2 years. You should do no more than 30 hours of childcare per week. If you are a native English speaker you will be encouraged to teach it too!
Getting started	Visit www.ufaap.org for the most recent list of approved *Au pair* agencies in France and lots of information in English.

Note: Although not exclusively the domain of women, men are rarely employed as *filles au pair,* in France or elsewhere.

5. Chèques emploi (CESU)

Translation	Employment vouchers
Description	A legal alternative to moonlighting.
Pros	An easy way to work for yourself without the stress of managing reams of paperwork. Unemployment cover.
Cons	Limited employment opportunities.
Suitable for	"Personal services" (Gardeners, cleaners, housekeepers, drivers, childminders, babysitters, DIY handymen, private tutors, personal trainers...)
VAT	Not eligible.
Earnings Limit	None.

Health,
Pension and
Social Security
contributions

Your employer can opt to pay you using prepay vouchers (*CESU préfinancé*), which they purchase at a price (around 80% higher than the face value of the cheque) that includes the cost of your social *charges* and are available in paper or electronic form. In order to be able to cash these vouchers you need to be enrolled with the centre for CESU refunds (see www.cr-cesu.fr).

Alternatively, your employer can pay you directly by cash, cheque or bank transfer and then declare your salary online (*CESU déclaratif*), paying your *charges* in a separate transaction. As a proportion of your total wage these social charges account for about 45% meaning you are fully covered for health, pension and social security. You need not concern yourself with them however – as the money you receive directly from your employer has already had these charges deducted.

Accounts

If you have accepted a *CESU préfinancé* voucher as payment you must ensure that it is cashed before the end of February of the next calendar year. Be sure to check the date of issue on the cheque when you accept it.

In the case of *CESU déclaratif*, you need to check regularly to ensure your employer has actually declared your earnings. You can do this by logging onto www.pajemploi.urssaf.fr, if you are supplying childcare services, or cesu.urssaf.fr for any other service you might be providing.

In either case your earnings will automatically appear on your annual tax return.

Other formalities

CESU préfinancé vouchers are usually sold only to employers with a company number, often intended for employees as perks, for which the company receives a 25% tax credit.

Anyone may pay you using the *CESU déclaratif* system: every month they are required to declare your salary at www.pajemploi.urssaf.fr, if you are

supplying childcare services, or at cesu.urssaf.fr –
for any other service you might be providing. At the
end of the year they can claim a household tax
credit of 50% against your wages. Note that with
declarative no actual vouchers are exchanged.

2nd job?	Yes. Compatible with all other forms of employment.
Getting started	In order to cash *CESU préfinancé* vouchers you need to sign up at the centre for CESU refunds (www.cr-cesu.fr). You don't need to take any action to benefit from the *CESU déclaratif* system –other than to explain how it works to your employer!
Closing down	No action required.

Vouchers, such as *CESU préfinancé*, are a common workplace perk in France because many employers offer them as compensation for low wages. Although employees are sometimes required to pay up to 60% of the face value of each voucher –they remain popular because employers can count them as part of their running costs rather than as wages-in-kind, thereby exonerating them from having to pay any *charges salariales* for the employee. In other words, payment by vouchers can raise the effective wage of an employee without raising an employer's payroll costs.

Although vouchers for dry-cleaning, gifts, books and travel exist, *Tickets Restaurant* are by far the most popular –because not only are they redeemable in thousands of restaurants across France they can also be used in many supermarkets and grocery stores to buy food. If you have your own business therefore, and are eligible to buy vouchers, it is worth investing as much money as you can in them in order to reduce your tax and *charges* burden. Note however managing directors and partners are barred from receiving vouchers, unless they own 50% or less of the business.

6.   Auto-entrepreneur

Also known as   Micro-entreprise

Translation   Self-employed

Description   Start-up freelance status

Pros   The easiest way to get started as a freelancer in
France. Simplified social security payments and
paperwork. All formalities can be dealt with online.
Easy to track your earnings. If you don't earn – you
don't pay. Easy to wind-up.

Cons   Pro-rata earnings limit. Not eligible for VAT.
Earnings taxed as percentage of turnover (not profit).
Certain trades excluded. No unemployment cover.
Unlimited liability.

Suitable for	Individuals and very small businesses with low turnover and minimal overheads. Attractive to teachers, students, retirees and the unemployed.
VAT	Not eligible.
Earnings limit	Turnover of 32900 € for a service, freelance or craft business or a turnover of 82200 € for a products/retail business. If you exceed this ceiling (*plafond*) you will lose the right to pay your taxes as-you-go and you must register for VAT. If you exceed the limit again in the following year you lose the right to operate as an auto-entrepreneur altogether and are automatically switched to EI *regime classique* from the 1st of January the following year, with no hope of return, even if your turnover should drop below the limit the following year.
Liability	Unlimited. Even if you close your business it is illegal to leave any outstanding debts unpaid, including your

own social/pension/health contributions. Heavy fines
or jail-time await those who do not pay.

Accounts   Monthly or quarterly online filing. Impossible to
claim running costs against taxes and social
contributions – so it is not cost effective to have an
accountant do it for you.

Tax statute   There are two different statutes depending upon your
activity.

• BIC for Industrial and commercial (product
based) businesses.

• BNC for service businesses, freelancers and
craftsmen.

You can opt to pay tax as-you-go (*micro-fiscal*)
provided your total household revenue does not
exceed 26,631 €. You pay 1.7% of turnover under
BIC or 2.2% under BNC. Otherwise you must fill out
an annual household tax return as usual and pay on
demand.

Wages	You cannot pay yourself a wage. All turnover is regarded as income. If you want to reinvest in your business – it's your loss!
Health, Pension and Social Security contributions	*Micro-social* pay monthly or quarterly scheme. No minimum payments unless you exceed the earnings limit. Freelancers must contribute 23.1% of turnover, while retail/commercial businesses must pay 13.4%. Includes CFP training contribution. Your pension fund is managed by CIPAV and your health fund by RSI.
Offset	None; however, the tax authorities attribute a percentage of your turnover as running costs: 50% for BIC and 34 % for BNC, with a minimum deduction of 305 €.
Other formalities	You cannot register to be auto-entrepreneur if your trade requires you to pay into a trade-specific pension or health fund. Specifically:

- Farming, agriculture and landscaping
- Legal practices
- Health and medicine workers

- Insurance resellers
- Chartered Accountants
- Property developers and estate agents
- Vehicle and accommodation rentals
- Professional artists and authors

If you are a sales agent, someone who negotiates and concludes contracts on behalf of others, you are required to register yourself with the *Registre Spécial des Agents Commerciaux* (RSAC). This can be done at the *Greffe du tribunal de commerce* (www.infogreffe.fr).

Craftsmen can opt out of the *Répertoire des métiers* (RM) trades database, and retailers from the Registre du commerce et des societies (RCS) – an exemption form is available to download from www.lautoentrepreneur.fr.

Your business details (Name, structure, NAF code, VAT number, registered address, and any registration numbers (SIRET/SIREN, RCS, RM, RSAC)) must appear on all company documentation, including website.

If you register to become auto entrepreneur and

register a turnover of zero for a period of 2 years your business will be automatically closed and you will be barred from opening under the statute for another 2 years.

2nd job?	Yes. Compatible with all other forms of employment, although you may need to ask for permission from your employer.
Getting started	First select the NAF code which is the closest match to your activity (see Appendix A: NAF codes). Visit www.lautoentrepreneur.fr or www.guichet-entreprises.fr to register your business.
Closing down	It is a simple matter of completing a *déclaration de cessation d'activité* (cessation of activity declaration) to wind-up your business. The form is available at www.lautoentrepreneur.fr.

While unarguably this is the easiest way to become self-employed in France, its attractiveness is perhaps offset by the rule that you must pay your dues as a percentage of your turnover, not your profits. One assumes that this is in order to let the state forego the need to audit anyone's expenditure, which could prove a costly process for the tax-payer. On the other hand, it also makes the rule book a lot thinner and the paperwork less daunting!

There is a chance then that your actual running costs are higher than the government offset, risking an effective tax on your profits of over 100%! This means auto-entrepreneur is only suited to trades where the costs can be passed on to the customer or where the overheads can be kept below the government *abattement* rate. You should therefore bill your customers with as many costs as you can, itemising each one and attaching a copy of the receipt as proof. These costs then do not need to be included in your sales figures.

One major advantage is that many of the prerequisites for regulated professions do not apply under the system, so you can start-up pretty much any business you want without fear of being stalked. You will however still be subject to any regulations required of your trade (such as health and safety etc.).

In your first year the earnings limit can be a problem. When you make your monthly or quarterly declarations you must ensure that you do not exceed to the pro-rata revenue limit for the year. For example, if you start your freelance business on the first of July, your turnover must not exceed 16,450 € (half of 32,900) by the end of the year. Delaying invoicing until the following year is the recommended strategy then.

If you exceed the earnings limit during the year and are forced to switch to *regime classique* you may immediately be liable to register for VAT as well as settle down-payments on estimated pension, health and social security contributions. In other words a nightmare could start to unfold *tout de suite*. It is wise then to keep an eye on your turnover and if, for whatever reason, you exceed, or are about to exceed, the limit you would be wise to consider closing the business before this situation arises. You could then reopen another *auto-entrepreneur* business with your social and tax commitments reset to zero, although this would require you to choose a different NAF code.

Now, although these caveats might put the fear of Beelzebub into you, it is worth remembering that exceeding these earning limits can actually be quite difficult if all of your business comes from France. As such, *auto-entrepreneur* is perfect for most freelancers and part-time workers.

Auto entrepreneur

7. Travailleur Indépendant

Also known as   EI (Entreprise Individuelle Regime Classique)

Translation   Independent professional / Freelancer

Description   The standard self-employed status for individuals in France.

Pros   Relatively easy to set up. Can register for VAT (TVA). No earnings limit.

Cons   Negative cash-flow. Most businesses under this system close within three to four years. No unemployment cover. Difficult to track your earnings. Unlimited liability.

Suitable for   Any activity guaranteeing a regular and stable monthly income.

VAT   Required if your turnover exceeds 32900 € for a service, freelance or craft business or 82200 € for a commercial, products, business. You may pay according to a 'simplified' system whereby you pay an estimated figure based on a fixed percentage (20%) of your turnover from two years previously as VAT, however if your income is not stable from year to year – you should opt to pay the 'real' VAT. You are required to settle VAT bills every quarter (in April, July, October and December).

Tax statute   There are three different statutes depending upon your activity. (see impots.gouv.fr for more details)

- BIC for Industrial and commercial businesses. Essentially for any non-agricultural commercial business selling tangible products.
- BNC for service businesses, craftsmen and freelancers.
- BA for agricultural businesses.

None of these statutes will make much difference to the amount of tax you pay.

Offset   34% under special BNC. Legislation changes
regularly as to what you can or can't claim as running
costs. It might be wise therefore to entrust your
accounts to a professional. See impots.gouv.fr for
more details.

Accounts   You should open a separate bank account through
which to process all your direct debits, invoices and
payments. Not only will this make your annual
accounts easier to compile it will also prevent the
state 'accidentally' taking money from you after you
close your business.

In the case of service businesses, if your turnover is
less than 32,900€ you may opt out of VAT and file
your accounts under *spécial BNC* – which lets you
claim 34% of turnover as costs without the need for
proof of expenditure. In this case you should be able
to complete all of your own paperwork online as you
won't be required to file your accounts with your
local tax office.

If your turnover exceeds 32,900€ however, it might be

wise to employ an accountant to help deal with the endless form-filling, bureaucracy and phone calls that the *déclaration controlee* requires.

Liability	Unlimited. Even if you close your business it is illegal to leave any outstanding debts unpaid, including your own social/pension/health contributions, even if they are based upon an incorrect estimate! Heavy fines or jail-time await those who do not pay. You may limit your liability by opting for EIRL status.
Wages	You cannot pay yourself a wage. All profits are regarded as taxable income. If you want to reinvest in your business you must do it by the end of the same fiscal year (i.e. before 31st December).
Certified Associations	If you are a member of a professional *Association Agréée* and have a reputable firm doing your books then you may get a tax reduction. See www.fnaga.com for more information.
Health,	Contributions for pension, health and social security

Pension and Social Security contributions

are calculated by estimating your coming year's earnings, using your earnings from two years previously as the basis. This means, unless you can maintain permanent stability of income or growth year-on-year, you will be forced to operate in a negative cash-flow environment, because you will have to start paying into these funds before you have even started earning. Freelancers should expect to pay approximately 40% of profits into these funds. Note there is a minimum contribution level of 1502 € per year. You can ask for a reduction of course, however even if your profit level is zero you will still be asked to part with at least 1185 €. If you have opted for complementary pension or health cover these figures will be higher (see www.rsi.fr for more details.)

The RSI offer a handy simulator to help predict how much you will be expected to pay per year. Note however, that you will be required to pay by monthly direct debit from the moment you start your business, meaning you will always be paying your dues in advance, rather than arrears. www.rsi.fr/simulateur-cotisations-sociales.html

To help get your business off the ground the first two years contributions are fixed, however the difference is recuperated in the third and fourth years so putting money aside is essential:

- Year 1: 2667 €
- Year 2: 3833 €
- Year 3: estimated based on year 1 profit plus balancing payment for actual year 1.
- Year 4: estimated based on year 2 plus balancing payment for actual year 2.

Demands for balancing payments are sent out in October and need to be settled by Christmas. Any over-payment, due to over-estimation of your earning capability by the state, will be refunded after two years; except in the case of pension contributions – which are not refunded under any circumstances – so they should be contested at the time of estimation.

You can declare your annual income and have your charges calculated automatically by registering at www.net-entreprises.fr.

Other formalities If you are setting up a retail business your name must be added to the *Registre du commerce et des societies* (RCS) at a cost of around 62 €. If you are a sales agent it is the *Registre spécial des agents commerciaux* (RSAC). This can be done at the Greffe du tribunal de commerce (www.greffes.com) for around 26 €.

If you are setting up as a craftsperson you must also added to the *Répertoire des métiers* (RM) trades database (at a cost of around 185 €) as well as complete a preparatory course of at least 30 hours. (www.artisanat.fr)

If you are VAT registered and have any service clients in the EU, who are also registered and therefore exempt from paying VAT, you must fill out a monthly DES customs declaration with the amount and VAT details of the client. (see https://pro.douane.gouv.fr/)

Your business details (Name, structure, NAF code, VAT number, registered address and any registration numbers address and any registration numbers

(SIRET/SIREN, RCS, RM, RSEIRL, RSAC)) must appear on all company documentation, including website.

Your spouse or partner is allowed to participate in the running of your business, however you will be required to pay additional *charges,* which will vary according to their status as either a 'collaborator' or an 'employee'.

2nd job?   No. If you are employed elsewhere then you would have to pay your social charges twice, meaning double pension, health and social security contributions. It may also lead you into a bureaucratic quagmire of perpetual paperwork.

Getting started   First select the NAF code which is the closest match to your activity (see Appendix A: NAF codes). Then check to see if your profession or trade is regulated in any way and that you meet the conditions of entry.

Visit www.guichet-entreprises.fr or your local *centre de formalités des enterprises* (CFE) office or website to obtain the appropriate forms to fill out as well as a list of any supporting documents you may be required to produce (e.g. passport, proof of address). The CFE will be one of the following depending upon your activity:

- Freelance *Professionnel Libérale* services go to URSSAF (cfe.urssaf.fr)
- For commerce go to the local Chamber of commerce and industry (www.cci.fr)
- For crafts go to the *Chambre de métiers et de l'artisanat* (www.artisanat.fr)
- For sales agents go to the *Greffe du tribunal de commerce* (www.greffes.com)
  Note: A sales agent is someone who negotiates and concludes contracts of any purchase, sale, rental or service on behalf of others; such as insurance or real estate.
- For agriculture go to the *Chambre d'agriculture* (www.chambres-agriculture.fr)

Closing down   You must declare your end of activities to your CFE and ask for a *certificate de radiation* to be issued.

It's cruel being self-employed at Christmas time. While towns and cities across France sparkle with fairy lights and seasonal cheer we freelancers are forced to stay at our desks and work through our numbers before even considering going out for a glass of *vin chaud*.

December 2009 was the end of my fourth full year in business in France and as usual I had managed to blissfully ignore all eleven reminders that I'd programmed into my computer to do my monthly accounts –before finally sitting down to iron out a biscuit-tin full of receipts. The task was not particularly notable in itself, being the usual battles of honesty verses bank balance. Should I claim for expenses that I had made while not actually working? Could I get away with off-setting a dirty weekend against tax for example? However, while this internal struggle busied my brain and my fingers, it failed to counter a growing sense of nausea and a little voice at the back of my mind whispering solemnly "it's all gone pear-shaped".

I knew the end of year figures were not going to look good, but this was the moment when I knew I would discover just how bad things were, in gory black and white. Yes, 2009 was going to display all the financial hallmarks of a business, not in decline, but in the dustbin. I had overseen what stock brokers would refer to as a 'basket case'.

To make matters worse, while I wouldn't count myself as particularly entrepreneurial, until this point I had been under the impression, nay illusion, that my business skills weren't all that bad. After all, I had managed my own businesses, in first the UK then France, for a good six years without seeing my family starve, have my house repossessed or have the bailiffs come knocking. I had usually made a modest profit year-on-year and prudently reinvested money back into the business to ensure its future and also to make certain that the taxman didn't take too big a bite. What then – had gone wrong?

When we made the move to France in 2006 the exchange rate, pounds to Euros was such that we could walk the streets of Strasbourg with a smug grin our faces. After all at 1.48 Euro to the pound – who wouldn't have? Every penny we shipped across the channel enabled us to finance a lifestyle that was a good one and a half times better than in England. How times change. While it was easy to predict the downfall of the UK's house of (credit) cards, the plummet in the value of Sterling came as a nasty shock, to us and most other expat Brits living in the Eurozone. Indeed it meant that many had to throw in the towel and move back to Blighty.

This reality for us also required a serious reassessment of our situation. I had been working for UK companies more or less perpetually since our arrival in France; billing in pounds and pence. Which meant in the short time that we'd been living there I'd had to mitigate against a slide of almost 33% in the value of my business, whilst operating within the inflexible confines of the French tax and social security systems.

Putting things into perspective, at least the bad news was expected this particular year. The previous year I had been close to cancelling Christmas after receiving a shock stack of bills from various French institutions demanding payment of some nine thousand Euro, which I was required to settle before Santa had packed his sleigh! The only surprise, as far as my accountant was concerned though, was that I hadn't expected this, and then … that he'd forgotten to tell me to do as much! This oversight did not result in a downward adjustment in his annual fee, however.

Festive celebrations that year were understandably low key. Soon after the children had unwrapped their yuletide lumps of coal and gorged themselves on beans-on-toast with all the trimmings I was forced to visit the bank manager to plead for that very un-French of financial facilities: credit. Had I still been in the UK this would not have been necessary. Even after the burst of the banking bubble in 2008, credit was still a relatively easy thing to acquire, provided of course you already had some. Asking for credit was one thing you certainly did not have to do. So the year started as it was destined to continue: in the red.

When I'd sat down with my accountant seven months earlier, to sign off the previous year's accounts, I'd taken the opportunity to quickly draw up a rough cash-flow chart, thinking that it might help him to find a solution to my predicament. The sudden drop in the value of the pound coupled with a drop in earnings were going to result in a net outflow of cash from me to *Monsieur le President* until the end of the year, leaving me, and my family, with practically nothing to live on.

"Well you know you should allow for around 35% of your earnings to be deducted" he crowed from inside his crisply ironed shirt.

"Fair enough" I replied, trying not to sound too pathetic, "but I appear to be paying between 50 and 60%?".

"Ah yes, well."

And then he gave me one of those famous Gallic shrugs, that when linguistically translated into English mean something along the lines of "I'm glad I'm not you, monkey-boy". The meeting ended amicably however, and I left with assurances that they would telephone all the necessary institutions to ask for restraint when leeching me of cash - until my official numbers had been filed at least. I was still going to be leeched throughout the rest of the year of course, but at least this time I would be prepared for it, and would know to restrain myself from impulse purchases of luxury items like food and electricity.

In actual fact the underlying issue to my predicament was not the collapse in the pound, but the French system itself; because, rather than settling your dues for pension, health and social security funds in arrears, in France you are required to pay before what you owe is even known. It's not unlike paying your electricity bill by direct-debit two weeks before you receive the bill – only to find that it's been wildly over estimated. Unlike your electricity payments however, errors of judgment by the French state cannot be corrected much before the end of the following financial year. Meaning the state gets to hold on to your money for up to two years, while you struggle to survive, before giving it back – without interest. What's worse, in the case of miscalculated pension contributions, you're not entitled to refunds at all. My crime was having spectacularly good second year followed by very mediocre third and fourth years.

It is an idiotic system dreamt up by someone who has clearly never tried to run their own business. All it does is ensures the government is never out of pocket. The only circumstances under which the « Travailleur Independent » system would work are those of an employee. In other words only with a guaranteed monthly income, perpetually stable or growing year on year, can you make it work. Monthly – because you're required to pay your dues every month, perpetually stable – because if your earnings drop year-on-year you will be stuck in negative cash-flow. Once I realised this – I shut up shop and tried to get a job instead. It was a difficult decision to make not least because proprietors of failed businesses are not entitled to unemployment benefit either!

I naïvely believed that this would mark an end to the incessant paperwork that comes with running your own business in *La Republique*. While on the upside it meant an end to demands for payment from the health, pension, social security, professional association and tax authorities, the downside was that it trapped me in a no-man's land of anonymity while I waited for all the various organisations to acknowledge the end of my affairs. A crucial document known as the *certificat de radiation* had to be issued before I could get a *certificat de fin de droits*, which would enable me to get an updated *attestation securité sociale* ... and so it went on; the whole process taking a good six months to rattle through the halls of power.

Today, I can look back at 2009, in good humour, as the year I learned a great deal about earning a living in France; at the time though, it was nothing short of a nightmare.

Note that the system of estimating future earnings, in order to calculate what you owe, is not just particular to the *Entreprise Individuelle* statute. If you opt for EIRL, EURL, SASU, SELARL or SELAS it is likely you will pay your dues according to a similarly demented schedule too. In which case you should make every effort to ring-fence approximately 50% of your monthly turnover (and VAT where applicable) to cover off the bills as they come in.

8.   Artiste-Auteur

Also known as   EI (Entreprise Individuelle Regime Classique)

Translation   Artist / Author

Description   Preferential status for artists and authors.

Pros   Lower social contributions and taxes. Can register for VAT. No earnings limit. Collect royalties.

Cons   Limited social cover until you gain affiliated status. No unemployment cover.

Suitable for   You are considered an artist-author if you create unique or limited-edition works of art, literature, music, choreography, film, photography, graphics, fine-arts or software. You are not considered an artist-author if you do any of these in conjunction with another activity.

VAT registration	Mandatory unless previous year's turnover was less than 42300€. You may pay according to a 'simplified' system whereby you pay a fixed percentage of your turnover as VAT (20%), however if you have foreign clients – you should opt to pay the 'real' VAT. You are required to pay VAT every quarter (in April, July, October and December).
Liability	Unlimited. Even if you close your business it is illegal to leave any outstanding debts unpaid, including your own social/pension/health contributions.
Tax statute	Regime Générale: Choose between special BNC (turnover must be less than 32,900 €) enabling a simplified filing, claiming 34% of turnover as costs, or *Déclaration contrôlée* which has the advantage that you can ask for your taxes to be averaged based on a two or four-year revenue period. To help get you started you are also entitled to a 50% reduction in tax during your first four

years. This statute suits those <u>not</u> represented by a publisher or gallery.

Regime Spéciale: 10% of turnover is claimed as costs. Your social security contributions are also deducted before your tax is calculated meaning you pay tax on about 75% of your income. This statute suits those represented by a publisher or gallery.

Accounts

Curiously, artists and authors work to a financial year that runs from July to June (although the tax year still runs from January to December – just to confuse you.) You need to declare your income before 15 April with AGESSA/Maison des artistes.

Wages

All profits are regarded as taxable income. If you want to reinvest in your art you must do it by the end of the same fiscal year (i.e. before 30th June).

Health, Pension and Social Security contributions

These are usually deducted at source by your publisher or gallery. As an *assujetti* you contribute approximately 10% of each sale for basic social security and health cover. You do not, however, get any sort of retirement package. Only once you are *affilié* do you start paying an additional 7% into a complementary retirement fund (IRCEC). Also, once affiliated, you are fully covered for social security and health.

If you are registered under the BNC statute or sell any work directly to customers, you will have to settle social contributions directly yourself every quarter (15 Jan, 15 Apr, 15 Jul and 15 Oct). These, however, are based on your previous year's earnings. If you fail to pay within one month of the deadline URSSAF, with whom you will have to negotiate if you want a reduction in your charges, will pursue you for settlement.

Other formalities

If you are VAT registered and have any service clients in the EU, who are also registered and therefore exempt from paying VAT, you must fill out a monthly DES customs declaration with the amount and VAT details of the client. (see https://pro.douane.gouv.fr/)

Your status as an artist or author is not permanent, every 18 months you have to provide proof of your activity, and that you are able to make money from doing it; a reason to keep your CV up to date!

Your details (Name, structure, NAF code, VAT number, registered address, and AGESSA/MdA number) must appear on all documentation, including website.

2nd job?　　Yes. Compatible with all other forms of professional employment.

Getting started　　You must first register as an artist or author with URSSAF at www.cfe.urssaf.fr or www.guichet-entreprises.fr – then once you have billed your first client you need to apply to be affiliated with either the Maison des artistes (for artists www.mda-securitesociale.org) or AGESSA (for authors www.agessa.org).

Once enrolled you are considered *assujetti* (subject) then if, by the end of your first year, you've earned at least 8,577 € from the sale of creative works you earn recognition as an artist or author which entitles you to become *affilié* (affiliated) with AGESSA or the Maison des Artistes. Note though that affiliation is not guaranteed, because your application to be an *artiste-auteur* is subject to approval by committee.

Closing down   You must declare your end of activities with URSSAF (cfe.urssaf.fr) and send a copy of the declaration to AGESSA/Maison des Artistes.

This variant of the Regime Classique, at just under seventeen percent, offers the lowest rate of social contributions across all forms of employment in France. One assumes this is due in no small part to the policies of "cultural exception" introduced by André Malraux in the fifties and sixties which were designed to defend the arts from foreign invaders. Happily nowadays you don't have to be French in order to benefit from the French Cultural Exception but you do have to be in France.

9.   Intermittent du spectacle

Translation   Performing arts contractor

Description   Status for performing arts professionals (technicians
                     and artists) experiencing periods of unemployment
                     between contracts

Pros   Can claim job-seekers allowance between contracts
                     which is paid relative to your previous income. (So
                     the more you earn –the more you're entitled to when
                     you're not earning!)

Cons   Difficult to get started. You must maintain regular
                     employment in order to retain your status.

Suitable for   Musicians, Models, Actors, Dancers, Voice Overs,
                     Backstage Crew, Film/Radio Editors, Radio Crew,
                     Sound Crew, Event/Show Crew, Set Builders, Disc
                     Jockeys, etcetera.

Earnings limit   4,438 € per month.

Accounts   You must declare your activities with Pole Emploi every month. Stating:

- The start and finish date of every contract
- The hours worked
- The number of fees (cachets)
- Gross wages excluding costs
- The name of the employer

Tax statute   Standard household tax rates apply

Health, Pension and Social Security contributions   Paid at source by your employers. Often deducted after an *abattement* to cover your costs. Effective total deductions account for around 20% of your gross wage.

Other formalities   As an *intermittent du spectacle* you are not, technically speaking, self-employed –because your employers pay your social security, pension and health contributions at the end of each contract.

Although not every employer you work for will be a recognised performing arts business they should be able to run the correct form of payroll for you by signing up to GUSO (www.guso.fr).

Should you work abroad for a non-French employer then the hours may not count towards the requisite 507 needed to maintain your status. You may also want to organise your own shows or performances; in which case –a common work-around to these problems is to create your own not-for-profit Association with which to employ yourself as an artist/technician for each project. Note though that you must not be the President of your own association – because Association Presidents are forbidden from drawing a wage!

You can find out more about setting up an association at www.associations.gouv.fr

---

2nd job?   No. The moment you find another form of employment you lose your right to unemployment benefit.

Getting started You need to be employed as an artist or technician for at least 507 hours over a period of 10 months in order to qualify for and maintain your status as an *intermittent du spectacle*. You must first be enrolled as a job seeker with Pole Emploi and aged under 60. (see www.pole-emploi.fr/informations/pole-emploi-spectacle-@/spectacle/ for more information.)

A good starting point at to find your first contract is the employment section of www.intermittent-spectacle.fr.

The existence of the *intermittent du spectacle* status is behind a thriving performing arts industry in France, by enabling crew and artists to benefit from a living wage in between contracts. Like the Artiste-Auteur status, it also offers recipients relatively low rate of social contributions (20%) although these are due to rise next year owing to pressure from other sectors of French industry, who believe that the system is not cost effective.

10. Portage Salarial

Translation	Umbrella company employee
Description	A stress-free, professional way to work for yourself
Pros	An easy system to use. Save time and look professional without the stress of managing a back-office. Unemployment cover. You can charge VAT. No nasty surprises: you pay your social security, health and pension contributions as you go, based on real earnings.
Cons	High running costs. Expenditure limited to 15% of turnover.
Suitable for	Home workers, consultants, designers, IT/web professionals, programmers, coders, life coaches, mixed-service businesses, etc.
Liability	Liability lies entirely with the company.

Earnings limit   None. However most portage firms will require you to provide proof of average earning capacity before sending you an employment contract.

VAT registration   All *portage* firms are VAT registered; you share the company's VAT number with everyone else registered with the firm.

The firm deals with all VAT related paperwork and payments, so there is no need to concern yourself with it. You won't see any direct rebate from your purchasing however; though the firm may indirectly reimburse you as part of your monthly expenses claim.

Accounts   The firm does not deal directly with your clients. You are required to liaise with your customers on all matters regarding contracts, orders and payments. Invoicing, account filing, reimbursement of expenses, tax returns, liability and payroll however are the responsibility of the *portage* company.

Every contract you undertake must be signed by

yourself, the client and a representative of the portage firm, this ensures it is legally binding. Each contract enables the issue of invoices – by the portage firm – which are then directly settled by your clients (i.e. the money goes into the firm's bank account, not yours.)

Every time the firm receives a payment from one of your clients they deduct their fee (a fixed percentage), and set aside the balance until you ask to be paid your salary (see below).

You can claim running costs up to a ceiling of 15% every month. These are deducted from the payroll before your wage is calculated.

Tax statute	You are considered an employee so you pay standard household income tax. Your earnings automatically appear on your annual tax return.
Wages	Every month you wish to be paid you should ask your portage firm to issue a CDD (*le contrat à durée déterminée*) for you to sign. This creates an employment period for which payroll can be run

85

using the balance of funds received from your clients, minus the portage firms' fees.

Your wages include a provision for holiday pay and *regularisation* of previous wages (meaning your pay may be adjusted up or down, month to month).

Health, Pension and Social Security contributions

Although you are officially an employee – you also settle the employer's contributions on your wage packet as well as your own (i.e. you pay both the *charges salariales* and *patronales* together).

You also pay into a whole range of funds that other employed people are exempt from, this means you pay more than the standard 35%.

Employee contributions will account for about 45% of gross salary and employer contributions for around another 20%. As an example, this would mean, if your portage firm charges 5% and you have no overheads to cover, that your total take home would be approximately 55% of your turnover.

Other formalities Portage firms usually charge their fees based on a sliding scale according to your revenue. For example, you might pay 5% up to a turnover of 100,000€ and then 2% thereafter. Some firms offer complementary healthcare and other peripheral benefits; however this usually means they charge more for their services (anything from 10% to 15% of turnover).

If your portage firm charges 10% or more your net take home is likely to be less than 50% of turnover, so it is best to choose a firm that offer lower rates.

You are regarded by the state as a full-time salaried worker. If your spouse works too this can be useful because it enables you to qualify for childcare and childminding places at crèches, playgroups and schools.

You can claim unemployment benefit between contracts if your last three months gross wage exceeded 2900€ per month.

Your details (Your name, portage company name, structure, NAF code, VAT number, current social capital, registered address and any registration numbers) must appear on all company documentation, including website.

2nd job? Yes. Compatible with all other forms of employment.

Getting started Update your CV and send it with a covering letter/email (preferably in French) to the portage firm of your choice. You can find a list of firms at www.guideduportage.com; be sure to check the management fee (*frais de gestion*) before requesting an employment contract. Percentages above 5% could prove costly. Do not feel obliged to choose the portage firm nearest to you or one that specialises in your skillset – they should all do more or less the same thing

---

Closing down No special action required.

I switched to *Portage Salarial* after the collapse of my EI *Travailleur Independent* business in 2010. Although admittedly I wave goodbye to some 45% of my turnover every month, it is not a decision I regret in the slightest. By placing a middle man between myself and the state I am relieved of having to deal with any of the back-office paperwork that caused me so much time, stress and cash as a *Travailleur Independent* (EI). I don't need to hire an accountant, file accounts or deal with customs declarations. It protects me from unexpected bills arriving two weeks before Christmas, cash-flow problems and, perhaps most importantly, from having to deal with any jobs-worth *functionnaires* (civil servants), of which there are many in France.

Portage salarial

11. CAE

Also known as	Coopératives d'activités et d'emploi
Translation	Workers Cooperative
Description	A testing bed for your entrepreneurial pursuits
Pros	Easy to reinvest in the business and grow. Functional, advisory and administrative support from other members of the cooperative. Workplace training opportunities. Earn a wage or work while claiming job seekers allowance.
Cons	Lengthy application procedure.
Suitable for	Artists, authors, craftspeople, builders, people providing services in the home, budding entrepreneurs looking for a safe way to test out their idea. Independent workers starting out on their careers.

Earnings limit   None

VAT registration   You share the cooperative's VAT number with the other members.

Liability   Liability lies entirely with the cooperative.

Accounts   You pay 10% of your turnover to the cooperative to take care of your accounts and payroll.

Tax statute   You are considered an employee so you pay standard household income tax. Your earnings automatically appear on your annual tax return.

Wages   Once you begin earning you are considered a salaried *entrepreneur*. Depending upon your situation, and the success of the cooperative, your wage may not be directly linked to your turnover as the cooperative's other activities, if profitable, may be sufficient to guarantee you a minimum wage, regardless of your success for any given month.

Health, Pension and Social Security contributions	Although you are officially an employee – you also settle the employer's contributions on your wage packet as well as your own (i.e. you pay both the *charges salariales* and *patronales* together).

Other formalities	If your business becomes a success you may be invited to become an associate partner of the cooperative and share in its other activities.

Your details (Your name, coop name, structure, NAF code, VAT number, current social capital, registered address and any registration numbers) must appear on all company documentation, including website. |

2nd job?	Yes. Compatible with all other forms of employment.

Getting started	You need to decide which category your activity fits into (generalist, building, culture or personal services) then consult the appropriate list of local cooperatives at www.cooperer.coop.

Once you have found a local coop you will need to attend a meeting to understand how they function. You then need to draw up a proposal for your "project" (in French ideally). After studying your proposal the cooperative will interview you and decide whether you can become a member.

You may be invited to begin working straight away or, if your project requires development before it can begin making you money, you may be asked to sign a CAPE (*contrat d'appui au projet d'entreprise*) which will enable you to operate under the structure of the cooperative, albeit unsalaried.

Closing down   No special action required.

What makes the CAE option interesting is that it doesn't put you under any pressure to begin earning immediately. With support, training and advice from other members of the cooperative you can work on your idea/product/service until it's ready to hit the market. Then, if your business becomes a success, you are not obliged to stay with the coop –you may leave and set up your own independent business, guilt free!

12. EIRL/AERL

Also known as   Entreprise Individuel/Auto Entrepreneur à
Responsabilité Limitée

Translation   Limited sole trader

Description   Lets you limit your liability under the *Regime
Classique* or *auto-entrepreneur* statuses. (See entries
for *auto-entrepreneur* and *Travailleur Independant*
above)

Pros   You won't lose your house should your business fail.
You can pay yourself a wage and reinvest in your
business.

Cons   Increased paperwork. Additional set-up and running
costs. Mandatory account filing. Cannot sell shares.
No unemployment cover.

Suitable for   Self-employed homeowners

Earnings limit   See entries for *auto-entrepreneur* and *Travailleur Independant* above.

Liability   Every year you have to declare all assets that are the property of the business as security against failure. These must have a value greater than zero in order to qualify for EIRL status. If you choose to include an item that is shared with a partner or spouse – you must have their written permission in order to do so. There is a fee of 56€ for filing your declaration of liability.

NB: Your stated liability cannot be used as a guarantee against a bank loan. If you borrow money from a bank you will be held personally liable for any non payment.

Accounts   You are required to open a separate bank account through which to process all your direct debits, invoices and payments.

Account filing is mandatory, so you are required to hire an accountant to draw up your annual reports.

Tax statute   Income Tax IR (*impôt sur la revenue*) *Classique* BNC, Micro BNC, BIC or BA depending on your legal statute (see entries for *auto-entrepreneur* and *Travailleur Indépendant* above).

or

Company Tax IS (*impôt sur les societies*) is also available to EIRL Freelancers who wish to reinvest some of their profits in the business. This is calculated at 15% up to a ceiling of 38,120 € and 33.33% thereafter.

Note that if you opt to pay IS you are prohibited from switching to IR at a later date.

Under this regime you can also pay yourself a dividend, however if the dividend is greater than 10% of your total liability or greater than 10% of annual profits – you will have to pay additional social contributions.

Wages   You may only pay yourself a wage under EIRL if you opt to pay company tax (*impôt sur les societies*). Your wage then is deductable from the business's profits.

Health, Pension and Social Security contributions	If you employ yourself your social security, pension and health contributions will be calculated according to your wage.
	If you are not registered to pay company tax (IS) then you will have to pay social security contributions based on the company profits as a *travailleur non-salariée* (TNS) by URSSAF. Meaning you will pay into the various funds as if you were a *travailleur indépendant* (see earlier section).
Other formalities	Your business details (Name, structure, NAF code, VAT number, registered address and any registration numbers (SIRET/SIREN, RCS, RM, RSEIRL, RSAC)) must appear on all company documentation, including website.
2nd job?	AERL – Yes. EIRL – No. However, there is nothing to stop you from running an EIRL while you are employed elsewhere.

Getting started See entries for *auto-entrepreneur* and *Travailleur Indépendant* above. When you set up your business through your CFE (or www.guichet-entreprises.fr) you should tick the EIRL option box on the form. Refer also to the Liability section above.

See www.eirl.fr for more information.

I have yet to meet anyone who has opted for this relatively new variant of the auto-entrepreneur and enterprise individuelle statutes. Created in 2012 it was designed to tackle the problem of the personal ruin often experienced as a direct result of business failure. Should your business collapse spectacularly, not losing your home is certainly a major benefit; however, it is widely believed that the rigidity and complexity of the legislation governing EIRL/AERL outweigh the benefits –which is why take-up, thus far, has been lackluster.

Crucially, under EIRL, you are still regarded as a *personne physique* (a person) – meaning your liability remains unlimited unless there is a clear demarcation between your personal and professional assets and affairs. Under the EURL and SASU statues however you can be considered a *personne morale* (a professional entity) – meaning you have no personal liability unless you use personal assets as a guarantee.

13. EURL

Also known as	Entreprise Unipersonnelle à Responsabilité Limitée
Translation	Limited sole proprietorship
Description	Basic private company status
Pros	Limited liability. You can employ staff, pay yourself a wage and reinvest company profits. Option to sell shares and switch to full company status (SARL) should the business grow.
Cons	Higher set up and running costs. Mandatory accounts and articles of association filing. More paperwork. No unemployment cover.
Suitable for	High earners.
Earnings limit	None.

VAT registration Mandatory. You may pay according to a 'simplified' system whereby you pay an estimated figure based on a fixed percentage (20%) of your turnover from two years previously as VAT, however if your income is not stable from year to year – you should opt to pay the 'real' VAT. You are required to settle VAT bills every quarter (in April, July, October and December).

If you are VAT registered and have any service clients in the EU, who are also registered and therefore exempt from paying VAT, you must fill out a monthly DES customs declaration with the amount and VAT details of the client. (see https://pro.douane.gouv.fr/)

Liability Limited to your capital. There must be a clear demarcation between your private assets and company assets and you should not put up any personal assets (such as your home) as guarantees against loans otherwise you will be held personally liable.

If you reinvest your profits into the business in the form of assets or cash you may increase your stated social capital accordingly.

Accounts   All your direct debits, invoices and payments must be processed through accounts attributed to the company. It is wise therefore to give the company a name other than your own!

Account filing is mandatory, so you are required to have an accountant draw up your annual reports.

If your turnover exceeds 3.1 million Euro, your profit exceeds 1.55 million Euro or you employ more than 50 people your accounts will need to be audited annually.

You must hold an Annual General Meeting with all your shareholders (i.e. you).

Tax statute   Income Tax IR (*impôt sur la revenue*) BNC, BIC or BA depending on your sector of activity.

or

Company Tax IS (*impôt sur les societies*) if you wish to reinvest some of the profits back into the business, employ people and pay yourself a wage. This is calculated at 15% up to a ceiling of 38,120 € and 33.33% thereafter.

Wages

You may only pay yourself a wage if you opt to pay company tax (*impôt sur les societies*). Your wage then is deductable from the company's profits.

If you pay company tax you may pay yourself a dividend, however if the dividend is greater than 10% of your total liability or greater than 10% of annual profits – you will have to pay additional social contributions. However, if these dividends account for less than 10% you will still have to contribute 15.5% in social charges.

Health, Pension and Social Security contributions

If you employ yourself your social security, pension and health contributions will be calculated according to your wage.

If you are not registered to pay company tax (IS) then you will have to pay social security contributions based on the company profits.

In either case you will be regarded as a *travailleur*

non-salariée (TNS) by URSSAF. Meaning you will pay into the various funds as if you were a *travailleur indépendant* (see earlier section). You will therefore not benefit from unemployment cover.

Other formalities

Your business details (Your name, company name, structure, NAF code, VAT number, current social capital, registered address and any registration numbers (SIRET/SIREN, RCS, RM, RSEIRL, RSAC etc.)) must appear on all company documentation, including website.

If you are a member of a professional *Association Agréée* and have a reputable firm doing your books then you may get a tax reduction. See www.fnaga.com for more information.

There are a number of activities prohibited from using the EURL status, namely: Insurance brokerage; Money lending and savings; Tobacconists.

Seeking investment

Should the situation arise whereby you need to start looking for some major financial backing you could upgrade your business to SARL status – which would allow you to start selling shares in the business. At this point however you would no longer be considered a freelancer or sole-proprietor.

2nd job?   No. However, there is nothing to stop you from running a EURL while you are employed elsewhere.

Getting started   First you must draw up your articles of association. These are basically the rules of governance of your company. There are a number of online templates to help you get started (see www.apce.com). Once filed, your details need to be published on BodAcc (see www.bodacc.fr) at a cost of 190€ and company registration with the RCS (*Registre du Commerce et des Sociétés*) costs around 84€.

Any money or assets you commit at the outset must be tangible to at least 20% of the promised full value in order to be considered social capital on the day of incorporation. The full amount has to be collected within 5 years.

Select the NAF code which is the closest match to your activity (see Appendix A: NAF codes). Then check to see if your profession or trade is regulated in any way and that you meet the conditions of entry.

Check that the company name you want to use is not already in use by searching through the online database at www.inpi.fr.

Visit www.guichet-entreprises.fr or your local *centre de formalités des enterprises* (CFE) office or website to obtain the appropriate forms to fill out as well as a list of any supporting documents you may be required to produce. The CFE will be your local chamber of commerce (www.cci.fr), *Chambre de métiers et de l'artisanat* (www.artisanat.fr) or *Chambre d'agriculture* (www.chambres-agriculture.fr) depending on your activity.

Closing down

This will depend on your reasons for closing down. You will either have to dissolve or liquidate the firm. You will need to send a *procès verbal* (legal statement) to the tax office, declare the end of your business with the CFE and *greffe du tribunal de commerce* as well as publish your cessation in the BodAcc. This process can be costly (over 1600€) and legally complex, but number of specialist companies exist to help people close down their businesses and ease the pain.

14. SASU

Also known as	Société par actions simplifiée unipersonnelle
Translation	Single proprietor public limited company
Pros	Limited liability. You can employ staff, pay yourself a wage and reinvest company profits. Option to sell shares and switch to full company status (SAS) should the business grow.
Cons	Higher set up and running costs. Mandatory account and articles of association filing. More paperwork. No unemployment cover.
Suitable for	Start-ups and entrepreneurs (in the true sense of the word)
Earnings limit	None

VAT Mandatory. You may pay according to a 'simplified' system whereby you pay an estimated figure based on a fixed percentage (20%) of your turnover from two years previously as VAT, however if your income is not stable from year to year – you should opt to pay the 'real' VAT. You are required to settle VAT bills every quarter (in April, July, October and December).

If you are VAT registered and have any service clients in the EU, who are also registered and therefore exempt from paying VAT, you must fill out a monthly DES customs declaration with the amount and VAT details of the client. (see https://pro.douane.gouv.fr/)

Liability Limited to your capital. There must be a clear demarcation between your private assets and company assets and you should not put up any personal assets (such as your home) as guarantees against loans otherwise you will be held personally liable.

If you reinvest your profits into the business in the form of assets or cash you may increase your stated social capital accordingly.

Accounts	If your turnover exceeds 2 million Euro, your profit exceeds 1 million Euro or you employ more than 20 people your accounts will need to be audited annually and write an annual report. You must file your accounts every year.
Tax statute	Company Tax IS (*impôt sur les societies*) calculated at 15% up to a ceiling of 38,120 € and 33.33% thereafter. Note you may instead opt for Income Tax IR (*impôt sur la revenue)* during the first five years only.
Wages	You can only draw a wage as an employee of a SASU (except if you have opted to pay IR in the first five years). You may pay yourself a dividend, however will have to contribute 15.5% of their value in social charges.
Health, Pension and	You are considered an employed partner (*assimilé-salarié*) so pay your contributions as an employee.

Social Security However, because you are your own employer – you
contributions are not entitled to unemployment cover.

Other formalities Your business details (Your name, company name,
structure, NAF code, VAT number, current social
capital, registered address and any registration
numbers (SIRET/SIREN, RCS, RM, RSEIRL, RSAC
etc.)) must appear on all company documentation,
including website.

Although a SASU is a public company – it cannot be
listed on the stockmarket.

There are two activities prohibited from using the
SASU status, namely:

- Agency for performing arts professionals (see
  Intermittent du spectacle)
- Tobacconist

2nd job? No. However, there is nothing to stop you from
running a SASU while you are employed elsewhere.

Getting started First you must draw up your articles of association.

These are basically the rules of governance of your company, but unlike the articles written for EURL, you are at liberty to include any number of clauses dictating how the company should operate. Once filed, your details need to be published on BodAcc (see www.bodacc.fr) at a cost of 230€ and company registration with the RCS (*Registre du Commerce et des Sociétés*) costs around 84€.

Any money or assets you commit at the outset must be tangible to at least 50% of the promised full value in order to be considered social capital on the day of incorporation. The full amount has to be collected within 5 years.

Select the NAF code which is the closest match to your activity (see Appendix A: NAF codes). Then check to see if your profession or trade is regulated in any way and that you meet the conditions of entry.

Check that the company name you want to use is not already in use by searching through the online database at www.inpi.fr.

Visit www.guichet-entreprises.fr or your local *centre*

de formalités des enterprises (CFE) office or website to obtain the appropriate forms to fill out as well as a list of any supporting documents you may be required to produce. The CFE will be your local chamber of commerce (www.cci.fr), *Chambre de métiers et de l'artisanat* (www.artisanat.fr) or *Chambre d'agriculture* (www.chambres-agriculture.fr) depending on your activity.

Closing down   This will depend on your reasons for closing down. You will either have to dissolve or liquidate the firm. You will need to send a *procès verbal* (legal statement) to the tax office, declare the end of your business with the CFE and *greffe du tribunal de commerce* as well as publish your cessation in the BodAcc. This process can be costly (over 1600€) and legally complex, but number of specialist companies exist to help people close down their businesses and ease the pain.

15. SELARL/SELAS

Also known as	Société d'Exercice Libéral : à Responsabilité Limitée (unipersonnelle) / par Actions Simplifiée
Translation	Private/Public non-commercial limited company
Description	Special company statuses for recognised professions.
Pros / Cons	For SELARL see above entry for EURL; for SELAS see above entry for SASU.
Suitable for	Architects; Auditors; Agriculture, land and forestry experts; Chartered Accountants; Dispensing Chemists; Doctors, dentists, mid-wives and other paramedical practices; High-street laboratories; Industrial Property Advisors; Law, legal and paralegal practices; Surveyors; Veterinarians
Earnings limit	None.

VAT registration	For SELARL see above entry for EURL; for SELAS see above entry for SASU.
Liability	For SELARL see above entry for EURL; for SELAS see above entry for SASU.
Accounts	For SELARL see above entry for EURL; for SELAS see above entry for SASU.
Tax statute	SELARL: If you have opted to pay IR (*impôt sur la revenue*) you may offset 10% against tax as running costs.
Wages	For SELARL see above entry for EURL; for SELAS see above entry for SASU.
Health, Pension and Social Security contributions	For SELARL see above entry for EURL; for SELAS see above entry for SASU.
Other formalities	You must be a recognised practitioner of the trade

under which you wish to launch your business. This means, even if you are recognised as a qualified professional in your home country, you must have your qualifications verified by the associated regulatory body. In many cases you may be required to acquire certified fluency in the French language and/or retrain in order to adapt your knowledge to the French market.

Equally, if you practice one of the regulated trades mentioned above you cannot open your business under SASU or EURL – being obliged to register under either SELAS or SELARL instead.

Although you can easily grow your business by selling shares, as the practitioner of the regulated trade, you are required to always retain and control at least 50% of the social capital.

If your business grows you do not need to change statute (as in the case of SASU and EURL).

2nd job?   No.

Getting
started

For SELARL see above entry for EURL; for
SELAS see above entry for SASU.

Closing down

For SELARL see above entry for EURL; for
SELAS see above entry for SASU.

Appendix A: NAF codes

When you register your business you may have to specify which, NAF code (*Nomenclature des Activités Françaises*), or APE code (*Activité Principale Exercée*), your activities will relate to, in order to reveal what type of business you will be doing. For example code 68.31Z indicates that you will be trading as a Real Estate Agent. This five-character code, four figures and a letter, besides statistical usefulness, indicates to INSEE (the national office of statistics) which institutions need to be notified of your activities when you register. Once registered, the appropriate Pension, Social Security and Health funds will contact you to acknowledge your registration and, if relevant, the appropriate trade body or regulator will also get in touch.

Once registered with INSEE, your name and address will be added to a national listing of companies and businesses which can be consulted by any member of the public. Unfortunately, this means you become an immediate target for junk mailing, sales calls and local teenagers looking for work experience.

It cannot be stressed enough then, that if you choose the wrong or an inappropriate NAF code, it could make life a little difficult. you can change your NAF code however, by calling or writing to

INSEE as soon as you have received your SIREN registration number.

There are currently seven hundred and thirty-two NAF codes to choose from. The below list was published by INSEE in 2008 (see recherche-naf.insee.fr). Here, an asterisk (*) indicates this may be a regulated profession – see Appendix B: Regulated professions and trades for more information.

SECTION A: AGRICULTURE, FORESTRY AND FISHING

01.11Z	Growing of cereals, leguminous crops or oil seeds
01.12Z	Growing of rice
01.13Z	Growing of vegetables, melons, roots or tubers
01.14Z	Growing of sugar cane
01.15Z	Growing of tobacco
01.16Z	Growing of fibre crops
01.19Z	Growing of other non-perennial crops
01.21Z	Growing of grapes
01.22Z	Growing of tropical and subtropical fruits
01.23Z	Growing of citrus fruits
01.24Z	Growing of nuts and stone fruits

SECTION A: AGRICULTURE, FORESTRY AND FISHING

01.25Z	Growing of other tree and bush fruits or nuts
01.26Z	Growing of oleaginous fruits
01.27Z	Growing of beverage crops
01.28Z	Growing of spices, aromatic, drug or pharmaceutical crops
01.29Z	Growing of other perennial crops
01.30Z	Plant propagation
01.41Z	Rearing dairy cattle
01.42Z	Rearing other cattle
01.43Z	**Rearing of horses and other equines***
01.44Z	Rearing camels
01.45Z	Rearing sheep and goats
01.46Z	Rearing swine/pigs
01.47Z	Rearing poultry
01.49Z	Rearing other animals
01.50Z	Mixed farming
01.61Z	Support activities for crop production
01.62Z	**Support activities for animal production***
01.63Z	Post-harvest crop activities

SECTION A: AGRICULTURE, FORESTRY AND FISHING

01.64Z	Seed processing for propagation
01.70Z	Hunting, trapping or related activities
02.10Z	Forestry activities
02.20Z	Logging
02.30Z	Gathering of wild non-wood plants/fungi
02.40Z	Forestry support services
03.11Z	Marine fishing
03.12Z	Freshwater fishing
03.21Z	Marine aquaculture
03.22Z	Freshwater aquaculture

SECTION B: MINING AND QUARRYING

05.10Z	Mining of hard coal
05.20Z	Mining of lignite
06.10Z	Extraction of crude oil
06.20Z	Extraction of natural gas
07.10Z	Mining of iron ores
07.21Z	Mining of uranium and thorium ores
07.29Z	Mining of other non-ferrous metal ores
08.11Z	Quarrying of ornamental building stone, limestone, gypsum, chalk or slate
08.12Z	Operation of gravel and sand pits; mining of clays and kaolin
08.91Z	Mining of chemical and fertiliser minerals
08.92Z	Extraction of peat
08.93Z	Extraction of salt
08.99Z	Other mining and quarrying
09.10Z	**Support activities for petroleum and natural gas extraction***
09.90Z	**Support activities for other mining and quarrying***

SECTION C: MANUFACTURING

10.11Z	**Processing and preserving of meat***
10.12Z	**Processing and preserving of poultry meat***
10.13A	Industrial production of meat products
10.13B	**Cooked meats production and trade***
10.20Z	Processing and preserving of fish, crustaceans and molluscs
10.31Z	Processing and preserving of potatoes
10.32Z	Manufacture of fruit and vegetable juice
10.39A	Other processing and preserving of vegetables
10.39B	Processing and preserving of fruit
10.41A	Manufacture of crude oils and fats
10.41B	Manufacture of refined oils and fats
10.42Z	Manufacture of margarine and edible fats
10.51A	Manufacture of milk or fresh dairy produce
10.51B	Manufacture of butter
10.51C	Manufacture of cheese
10.51D	Manufacture of other dairy products
10.52Z	**Manufacture of ice cream***
10.61A	Flour milling

SECTION C: MANUFACTURING

10.61B	Manufacture of other milled grain products
10.62Z	Manufacture of starches or starch products
10.71A	Industrial manufacture of bread or fresh pastry
10.71B	Baking of bakery products
10.71C	**Bakery and bakery confectionery***
10.71D	**Confectionery***
10.72Z	Manufacture of biscuits, preserved pastry goods or cakes
10.73Z	Manufacture of pasta, couscous or similar farinaceous products
10.81Z	Manufacture of sugar
10.82Z	**Manufacture of cocoa, chocolate or confectionery***
10.83Z	Processing of tea or coffee
10.84Z	Manufacture of condiments and seasonings
10.85Z	Manufacture of prepared meals and dishes
10.86Z	Manufacture of homogenised or dietetic food
10.89Z	Manufacture of other food products
10.91Z	Manufacture of feeds for farm animals
10.92Z	Manufacture of pet foods
11.01Z	Distilling, maturing and blending of spirits

SECTION C: MANUFACTURING

11.02A	Manufacture of sparkling wines
11.02B	Wine-making
11.03Z	Manufacture of cider and other fruit wines
11.04Z	Manufacture of other non-distilled fermented beverages
11.05Z	Manufacture of beer
11.06Z	Manufacture of malt
11.07A	**Production of mineral water***
11.07B	Production of soft drinks
12.00Z	Manufacture of tobacco products
13.10Z	Preparation and spinning of textile fibres
13.20Z	Weaving of fabrics
13.30Z	Finishing of fabric
13.91Z	Manufacture of knitted and crocheted fabrics
13.92Z	Manufacture of fabric articles, except apparel
13.93Z	Manufacture of carpets and rugs
13.94Z	Manufacture of cordage, rope, twine and netting
13.95Z	Manufacture of non-woven articles except apparel
13.96Z	Manufacture of other technical and industrial textiles

SECTION C: MANUFACTURING

13.99Z	Manufacture of other textiles
14.11Z	Manufacture of leather clothes
14.12Z	Manufacture of work wear
14.13Z	Manufacture of other outerwear
14.14Z	Manufacture of underwear
14.19Z	Manufacture of other wearing apparel and accessories
14.20Z	Manufacture of articles of fur
14.31Z	Manufacture of knitted and crocheted hosiery
14.39Z	Manufacture of other knitted and crocheted apparel
15.11Z	Tanning and dressing of leather; dressing and dyeing of fur
15.12Z	Manufacture of luggage, bags and saddlery
15.20Z	Manufacture of footwear
16.10A	Sawmilling and planing of wood
16.10B	Treating of wood
16.21Z	Manufacture of veneers and wood-based panels
16.22Z	Manufacture of parquet floors
16.23Z	Manufacture of other joinery
16.24Z	Manufacture of wooden containers

SECTION C: MANUFACTURING

16.29Z	Manufacture of other wooden products
17.11Z	Manufacture of pulp
17.12Z	Manufacture of paper and cardboard
17.21A	Manufacture of corrugated cardboard
17.21B	Manufacture of cardboard and cardboard boxes
17.21C	Manufacture of paper boxes
17.22Z	Manufacture of hygienic tissue papers
17.23Z	Manufacture of paper stationery
17.24Z	Manufacture of wallpaper
17.29Z	Manufacture of other articles of paper and cardboard
18.11Z	Printing of newspapers
18.12Z	Other printing
18.13Z	Pre-press and pre-media services
18.14Z	Binding and related services
18.20Z	Reproduction of recorded media
19.10Z	Manufacture of coke oven products
19.20Z	Manufacture of refined petroleum products
20.11Z	Manufacture of industrial gases

SECTION C: MANUFACTURING

20.12Z	Manufacture of dyes and pigments
20.13A	Enrichment and reprocessing of nuclear fuel
20.13B	Manufacture of other inorganic basic chemicals
20.14Z	Manufacture of other organic basic chemicals
20.15Z	Manufacture of fertilisers and nitrogen compounds
20.16Z	Manufacture of plastics in primary forms
20.17Z	Manufacture of synthetic rubber in primary forms
20.20Z	Manufacture of pesticides and other agrochemical products
20.30Z	Manufacture of coatings, inks and mastics
20.41Z	Manufacture of detergents and polishing preparations
20.42Z	Manufacture of perfumes and scents
20.51Z	Manufacture of explosives
20.52Z	Manufacture of glues
20.53Z	Manufacture of essential oils
20.59Z	Manufacture of other chemical products
20.60Z	Manufacture of man-made fibres
21.10Z	Manufacture of basic pharmaceutical products
21.20Z	Manufacture of pharmaceutical preparations

SECTION C: MANUFACTURING

22.11Z	Manufacture and retreading of rubber tyres and tubes
22.19Z	Manufacture of other rubber products
22.21Z	Manufacture of plastic plates, sheets and tubes
22.22Z	Manufacture of plastic packing
22.23Z	Manufacture of plastic building materials
22.29A	Manufacture of plastic parts
22.29B	Manufacture of plastic consumer goods
23.11Z	Manufacture of sheet glass
23.12Z	Shaping and processing of sheet glass
23.13Z	Manufacture of hollow glass
23.14Z	Manufacture of glass fibres
23.19Z	Manufacture and processing of other glassware
23.20Z	Manufacture of refractory products
23.31Z	Manufacture of ceramic tiles
23.32Z	Manufacture of baked clay bricks and tiles
23.41Z	Manufacture of ceramic articles
23.42Z	Manufacture of ceramic sanitary fixtures
23.43Z	Manufacture of ceramic insulators and insulating fittings

SECTION C: MANUFACTURING

23.44Z	Manufacture of other technical ceramic products
23.49Z	Manufacture of other ceramic products
23.51Z	Manufacture of cement
23.52Z	Manufacture of lime and plaster
23.61Z	Manufacture of concrete products for construction purposes
23.62Z	Manufacture of plaster products for construction purposes
23.63Z	Manufacture of ready-mixed concrete
23.64Z	Manufacture of mortars
23.65Z	Manufacture of fibre cement
23.69Z	Manufacture of other articles of concrete, plaster and cement
23.70Z	**Cutting, shaping and finishing of stone***
23.91Z	Production of abrasive products
23.99Z	Manufacture of other non-metallic mineral products
24.10Z	Manufacture of iron or steel based alloys
24.20Z	Manufacture of steel tubes, pipes and fittings
24.31Z	Cold drawing of bars
24.32Z	Cold rolling of narrow strips
24.33Z	Cold forming or folding

SECTION C: MANUFACTURING

24.34Z	Cold drawing of wire
24.41Z	Precious metals production
24.42Z	Aluminium production
24.43Z	Lead, zinc and tin production
24.44Z	Copper production
24.45Z	Other non-ferrous metal production
24.46Z	Processing of nuclear fuel
24.51Z	Casting of iron
24.52Z	Casting of steel
24.53Z	Casting of light metals
24.54Z	Casting of other non-ferrous metals
25.11Z	Manufacture of metal structures
25.12Z	Manufacture of metal doors and windows
25.21Z	Manufacture of central heating radiators and boilers
25.29Z	Manufacture of other metal tanks, reservoirs and containers
25.30Z	Manufacture of steam generators
25.40Z	Manufacture of weapons and ammunition
25.50A	Forging, pressing, stamping; powder metallurgy

SECTION C: MANUFACTURING

25.50B	Cutting out, pressing
25.61Z	Treatment and coating of metals
25.62A	Trimming
25.62B	Industrial mechanical engineering
25.71Z	Manufacture of cutlery
25.72Z	Manufacture of locks and hinges
25.73A	Manufacture of moulds and models
25.73B	Manufacture of other tools
25.91Z	Manufacture of steel drums and similar containers
25.92Z	Manufacture of light metal packaging
25.93Z	Manufacture of wire products, chain and springs
25.94Z	Manufacture of fasteners
25.99A	**Manufacture of household metal articles***
25.99B	Manufacture of other metal articles
26.11Z	Manufacture of electronic components
26.12Z	Manufacture of circuit boards
26.20Z	Manufacture of computers and peripheral equipment
26.30Z	Manufacture of communications equipment

SECTION C: MANUFACTURING

26.40Z	Manufacture of consumer electronics
26.51A	Manufacture of navigation equipment
26.51B	Manufacture of scientific and technical instruments
26.52Z	**Manufacture of watches and clocks***
26.60Z	Manufacture of irradiation, electro-medical and electrotherapeutic equipment
26.70Z	Manufacture of optical instruments and photographic equipment
26.80Z	Manufacture of magnetic and optical media
27.11Z	Manufacture of electric motors, generators and transformers
27.12Z	Manufacture of electricity distribution and control apparatus
27.20Z	Manufacture of batteries and accumulators
27.31Z	Manufacture of fibre optic cables
27.32Z	Manufacture of other electronic or electric wires and cables
27.33Z	Manufacture of wiring devices
27.40Z	Manufacture of electric lighting equipment
27.51Z	Manufacture of electric domestic appliances
27.52Z	Manufacture of non-electric domestic appliances
27.90Z	Manufacture of other electrical equipment

SECTION C: MANUFACTURING

28.11Z	Manufacture of engines and turbines
28.12Z	Manufacture of hydraulic equipment
28.13Z	Manufacture of other pumps and compressors
28.14Z	Manufacture of other taps and valves
28.15Z	Manufacture of bearings, gears, gearing and drive elements
28.21Z	Manufacture of ovens, furnaces and furnace burners
28.22Z	Manufacture of lifting and handling equipment
28.23Z	Manufacture of office machinery and equipment
28.24Z	Manufacture of power tools
28.25Z	Manufacture of non-domestic cooling and ventilation equipment
28.29A	Manufacture of packing and weighing equipment
28.29B	Manufacture of other general purpose machinery
28.30Z	Manufacture of agricultural and forestry machinery
28.41Z	Manufacture of machine-tools for metal work
28.49Z	Manufacture of other machine tools
28.91Z	Manufacture of machinery for metallurgy
28.92Z	Manufacture of machinery for mining, quarrying and construction
28.93Z	Manufacture of machinery for food, beverage and tobacco

	processing
28.94Z	Manufacture of machinery for textile, apparel and leather production
28.95Z	Manufacture of machinery for paper and cardboard production
28.96Z	Manufacture of plastics and rubber machinery
28.99A	Manufacture of printing machinery
28.99B	Manufacture of other special purpose machinery
29.10Z	Manufacture of motor vehicles
29.20Z	Manufacture of bodywork and trailers for motor vehicles
29.31Z	Manufacture of electrical and electronic equipment for motor vehicles
29.32Z	Manufacture of other parts and accessories for motor vehicles
30.11Z	Building of ships and floating structures
30.12Z	Building of pleasure and sports boats
30.20Z	Manufacture of railway locomotives and rolling stock
30.30Z	Manufacture of air and spacecraft and related machinery
30.40Z	Manufacture of military fighting vehicles
30.91Z	Manufacture of motorcycles
30.92Z	Manufacture of bicycles and invalid carriages

SECTION C: MANUFACTURING

30.99Z	Manufacture of other transport equipment
31.01Z	Manufacture of office and shop furniture
31.02Z	Manufacture of kitchen furniture
31.03Z	Manufacture of mattresses
31.09A	Manufacture of home furnishing chairs and seats
31.09B	Manufacture of other furniture and industry closely related to furnishing
32.11Z	Minting of coins
32.12Z	**Manufacture of jewellery and related articles***
32.13Z	**Manufacture of imitation jewellery and related articles***
32.20Z	Manufacture of musical instruments
32.30Z	Manufacture of sports goods
32.40Z	Manufacture of games and toys
32.50A	**Manufacture of medical, surgical and dental equipment***
32.50B	**Manufacture of glasses***
32.91Z	Manufacture of brooms and brushes
32.99Z	Other manufacturing
33.11Z	Repair of fabricated metal products

SECTION C: MANUFACTURING

33.12Z	Repair of machinery
33.13Z	Repair of electronic and optical equipment
33.14Z	Repair of electrical equipment
33.15Z	Repair and maintenance of ships and boats
33.16Z	Repair and maintenance of aircraft and spacecraft
33.17Z	Repair and maintenance of other transport equipment
33.19Z	Repair of other equipment
33.20A	Installation of metallic, boiler structures and pipes
33.20B	Installation of machinery and mechanical equipment
33.20C	Overall conception and assembly of industrial process control equipment in industrial plants
33.20D	Installation of electrical equipment, electronic and optical equipment or other equipment

SECTION D: ELECTRICITY, GAS, STEAM AND AIR CONDITIONING SUPPLY

35.11Z	Production of electricity
35.12Z	Transmission of electricity
35.13Z	Distribution of electricity
35.14Z	Trade of electricity

SECTION D: ELECTRICITY, GAS, STEAM AND AIR CONDITIONING SUPPLY

35.21Z	Manufacture of gas
35.22Z	Distribution of gaseous fuels
35.23Z	Trade of gas
35.30Z	Steam and air conditioning supply

SECTION E: WATER SUPPLY; SEWERAGE, WASTE MANAGEMENT AND REMEDIATION ACTIVITIES

36.00Z	Water collection, treatment and supply
37.00Z	Sewerage
38.11Z	Collection of non-hazardous waste
38.12Z	Collection of hazardous waste
38.21Z	Treatment and disposal of non-hazardous waste
38.22Z	Treatment and disposal of hazardous waste
38.31Z	Dismantling of wrecks
38.32Z	Recovery of sorted materials
39.00Z	Remediation activities and other waste management services

SECTION F: CONSTRUCTION

41.10A	Development and selling of dwellings
41.10B	Development and selling of offices
41.10C	Development and selling of other buildings
41.10D	Juridical compartmentalisation of property programmes
41.20A	Construction of detached and semi-detached houses
41.20B	Construction of other buildings
42.11Z	Construction of roads and motorways
42.12Z	Construction of railways and underground railways
42.13A	Construction of civil engineering structures
42.13B	Construction and maintenance of tunnels
42.21Z	Construction of utility projects for fluids
42.22Z	Construction of utility projects for electricity and telecommunications
42.91Z	Construction of water projects
42.99Z	Construction of other civil engineering projects
43.11Z	**Demolition***
43.12A	**Standard earth moving and preparation works***
43.12B	**Specialized earth moving***

SECTION F: CONSTRUCTION

43.13Z	Test drilling and boring
43.21A	Installation works of electrical wiring and fittings
43.21B	Electrical installation works on public thoroughfare
43.22A	Water and gas installation works
43.22B	**Installation of heating and air conditioning equipment (HVAC)***
43.29A	**Insulation work activities***
43.29B	**Other building installation works ***
43.31Z	**Plastering***
43.32A	**Wood and PVC joinery works***
43.32B	**Metal joinery works and ironwork***
43.32C	Finishing of sale premises
43.33Z	**Floor and wall covering***
43.34Z	**Painting and glazing***
43.39Z	Other building completion and finishing
43.91A	**Roof frames works***
43.91B	**Roof covering activities by elements***
43.99A	**Waterproofing***
43.99B	**Assembly works of metal structures***

SECTION F: CONSTRUCTION

43.99C	**Masonry works and building structural works***
43.99D	**Other construction works involving special trades***
43.99E	Renting of construction equipment with operator

SECTION G: WHOLESALE AND RETAIL TRADE; REPAIR OF MOTOR VEHICLES AND MOTORCYCLES

45.11Z	Sale of cars and light motor vehicles
45.19Z	Sale of other motor vehicles
45.20A	**Maintenance and repair of light motor vehicles***
45.20B	**Maintenance and repair of other motor vehicles***
45.31Z	Wholesale trade of motor vehicle parts and accessories
45.32Z	Retail trade of motor vehicle parts and accessories
45.40Z	Sale, maintenance and repair of motorcycles and parts
46.11Z	Agents involved in the sale of agricultural raw materials, live animals, textile raw materials and semi-finished goods
46.12A	Automotive fuel buying groups
46.12B	Agents for the sale of fuels, ores, metals and industrial chemicals
46.13Z	Agents involved in the sale of timber and building materials
46.14Z	Agents involved in the sale of machinery, industrial equipment, ships and aircraft

SECTION G: WHOLESALE AND RETAIL TRADE; REPAIR OF MOTOR VEHICLES AND MOTORCYCLES

46.15Z	Agents involved in the sale of furniture, household goods, hardware and ironmongery
46.16Z	Agents involved in the sale of textiles, clothing, fur, footwear and leather goods
46.17A	Food buying groups
46.17B	**Other agents involved in the sale of food, beverages and tobacco***
46.18Z	**Agents specialised in the sale of other particular products***
46.19A	Non food buying groups
46.19B	Other agents involved in the sale of a variety of goods
46.21Z	Wholesale of grain, unmanufactured tobacco, seeds and animal feeds
46.22Z	**Wholesale of flowers and plants***
46.23Z	Wholesale of live animals
46.24Z	Wholesale of hides, skins and leather
46.31Z	**Wholesale of fruit and vegetables***
46.32A	**Wholesale of fresh meat***
46.32B	**Wholesale of meat products***
46.32C	**Wholesale of poultry and game***
46.33Z	**Wholesale of dairy products, eggs and edible oils and fats***

SECTION G: WHOLESALE AND RETAIL TRADE; REPAIR OF MOTOR VEHICLES AND MOTORCYCLES

46.34Z	**Wholesale of beverages***
46.35Z	**Wholesale of tobacco products***
46.36Z	**Wholesale of sugar and chocolate and confectionery***
46.37Z	**Wholesale of coffee, tea, cocoa and spices***
46.38A	**Wholesale of fish, crustaceans and molluscs***
46.38B	**Wholesale of sundry food***
46.39A	**Wholesale of frozen products***
46.39B	**Wholesale of food, non specialized***
46.41Z	Wholesale of textiles
46.42Z	Wholesale of clothing and footwear
46.43Z	Wholesale of electrical household appliances
46.44Z	Wholesale of china and glassware and cleaning materials
46.45Z	Wholesale of perfume and cosmetics
46.46Z	Wholesale of pharmaceutical goods
46.47Z	Wholesale of furniture, carpets and lighting equipment
46.48Z	Wholesale of watches and jewellery
46.49Z	**Wholesale of other household goods***

SECTION G: WHOLESALE AND RETAIL TRADE; REPAIR OF MOTOR VEHICLES AND MOTORCYCLES

46.51Z	Wholesale of computers, peripheral equipment and software
46.52Z	Wholesale of electronic and telecommunications equipment
46.61Z	Wholesale of agricultural machinery, equipment and supplies
46.62Z	Wholesale of machine tools
46.63Z	Wholesale of mining, construction and engineering machinery
46.64Z	Wholesale of machinery for the textile industry and of sewing and knitting machines
46.65Z	Wholesale of office furniture
46.66Z	Wholesale of other office machinery and equipment
46.69A	Wholesale of electric equipment
46.69B	Wholesale of sundry industrial supplies and equipment
46.69C	Wholesale of sundry supplies and equipment
46.71Z	Wholesale of solid, liquid and gaseous fuels and related products
46.72Z	Wholesale of metals and metal ores
46.73A	Wholesale of wood and construction materials
46.73B	Wholesale of sanitary equipment
46.74A	Wholesale of hardware
46.74B	Wholesale of plumbing and heating equipment and supplies

SECTION G: WHOLESALE AND RETAIL TRADE; REPAIR OF MOTOR VEHICLES AND MOTORCYCLES

46.75Z	Wholesale of chemical products
46.76Z	Wholesale of other intermediate products
46.77Z	Wholesale of waste and scrap
46.90Z	Non-specialised wholesale trade
47.11A	**Retail sale of frozen products***
47.11B	**General food retail stores***
47.11C	**Mini-markets***
47.11D	**Supermarkets***
47.11E	**Multi-trade stores***
47.11F	**Hypermarkets***
47.19A	**Department stores***
47.19B	**Other retail sale in non specialized stores***
47.21Z	**Retail sale of fruit and vegetables in specialised stores***
47.22Z	**Retail sale of meat and meat products in specialised stores***
47.23Z	**Retail sale of fish, crustaceans and molluscs in specialised stores***
47.24Z	**Retail sale of bread, cakes, flour confectionery and sugar confectionery in specialised stores***
47.25Z	**Retail sale of beverages in specialised stores***

SECTION G: WHOLESALE AND RETAIL TRADE; REPAIR OF MOTOR VEHICLES AND MOTORCYCLES

47.26Z	**Retail sale of tobacco products in specialised stores***
47.29Z	**Other retail sale of food in specialised stores***
47.30Z	Retail sale of automotive fuel in specialised stores
47.41Z	Retail sale of computers, peripheral units and software in specialised stores
47.42Z	Retail sale of telecommunications equipment in specialised stores
47.43Z	Retail sale of audio and video equipment in specialised stores
47.51Z	Retail sale of textiles in specialised stores
47.52A	Retail sale of hardware, paints and glass in small stores (less than 400 m2)
47.52B	Retail sale of hardware, paints and glass in DIY superstores (400 m2 and more)
47.53Z	Retail sale of carpets, rugs, wall and floor coverings in specialised stores
47.54Z	Retail sale of electrical household appliances in specialised stores
47.59A	Retail sale of furniture
47.59B	Retail sale of other household equipment and articles
47.61Z	Retail sale of books in specialised stores
47.62Z	**Retail sale of newspapers and stationery in specialised stores***
47.63Z	Retail sale of music and video recordings in specialised stores

SECTION G: WHOLESALE AND RETAIL TRADE; REPAIR OF MOTOR
VEHICLES AND MOTORCYCLES

47.64Z	Retail sale of sporting equipment in specialised stores
47.65Z	Retail sale of games and toys in specialised stores
47.71Z	Retail sale of clothing in specialised stores
47.72A	Retail sale of footwear
47.72B	Retail sale of fine leather goods and of travel articles
47.73Z	**Dispensing chemist in specialised stores***
47.74Z	Retail sale of medical and orthopaedic goods in specialised stores
47.75Z	Retail sale of cosmetic and toilet articles in specialised stores
47.76Z	**Retail sale of flowers, plants, seeds, fertilisers, pet animals and pet food in specialised stores***
47.77Z	**Retail sale of watches and jewellery in specialised stores***
47.78A	**Retail sale of optics***
47.78B	**Retail sale of coal and fuels**
47.78C	**Other sundry specialized retail sale***
47.79Z	**Retail sale of second-hand goods in stores***
47.81Z	**Retail sale via stalls and markets of food, beverages and tobacco products***
47.82Z	Retail sale via stalls and markets of textiles, clothing and footwear

SECTION G: WHOLESALE AND RETAIL TRADE; REPAIR OF MOTOR VEHICLES AND MOTORCYCLES

47.89Z	Retail sale via stalls and markets of other goods
47.91A	Retail sale via home-shopping by general catalogue
47.91B	Retail sale via home-shopping by specialized catalogue
47.99A	From door to door sale
47.99B	**Vending machine sale and sundry retail trade not in stores, stalls or markets***

SECTION H: TRANSPORTATION AND STORAGE

49.10Z	Passenger rail transport, interurban
49.20Z	Freight rail transport
49.31Z	Urban and suburban passenger land transport
49.32Z	**Taxi operation***
49.39A	Road scheduled passengers land transport
49.39B	Other land passenger transport*
49.39C	Cableway and ski lifts
49.41A	**Interurban freight transport by road***
49.41B	**Proximity freight transport by road***
49.41C	**Rent of lorries with driver***

SECTION H: TRANSPORTATION AND STORAGE

49.42Z	**Removal services***
49.50Z	Transport via pipeline
50.10Z	Sea and coastal passenger water transport
50.20Z	Sea and coastal freight water transport
50.30Z	Inland passenger water transport
50.40Z	Inland freight water transport
51.10Z	Passenger air transport
51.21Z	Freight air transport
51.22Z	Space transport
52.10A	Refrigerated warehousing and storage
52.10B	Non refrigerated warehousing and storage
52.21Z	Service activities incidental to land transportation
52.22Z	Service activities incidental to water transportation
52.23Z	Service activities incidental to air transportation
52.24A	Harbour cargo handling
52.24B	Non harbour cargo handling
52.29A	**Freight services organization***
52.29B	**Chartering and transportation organisation***

53.10Z   Postal activities under universal service obligation

53.20Z   Other postal and courier activities*

SECTION I: ACCOMMODATION AND FOOD SERVICE ACTIVITIES

55.10Z	**Hotels and similar accommodation***
55.20Z	**Holiday and other short-stay accommodation***
55.30Z	**Camping grounds, recreational vehicle parks and trailer parks***
55.90Z	Other accommodation
56.10A	**Traditional catering***
56.10B	Cafeterias and other self-service catering
56.10C	**Fast food restaurants***
56.21Z	Event catering activities
56.29A	Collective catering under contract
56.29B	Other catering
56.30Z	**Beverage serving activities***

SECTION J: INFORMATION AND COMMUNICATION

58.11Z	**Book publishing***
58.12Z	Publishing of directories and mailing lists
58.13Z	**Publishing of newspapers***
58.14Z	**Publishing of journals and periodicals***
58.19Z	Other publishing activities

SECTION J: INFORMATION AND COMMUNICATION

58.21Z	Publishing of computer games
58.29A	System and network software publishing
58.29B	Development tools and programming languages software publishing
58.29C	Application software publishing
59.11A	Production of motion pictures for television and television programmes
59.11B	Production of institutional and promotional motion pictures
59.11C	Production of motion pictures for cinema
59.12Z	Motion picture, video and television programme post-production activities
59.13A	Motion pictures for cinema distribution
59.13B	Video edition and distribution
59.14Z	Motion picture projection activities
59.20Z	Sound recording and music publishing activities
60.10Z	**Radio broadcasting***
60.20A	Broadcast of general-interest television programmes
60.20B	Broadcast of thematic television programmes
61.10Z	Wired telecommunications activities
61.20Z	Wireless telecommunications activities

SECTION J: INFORMATION AND COMMUNICATION

61.30Z	Satellite telecommunications activities
61.90Z	Other telecommunications activities
62.01Z	Computer programming activities
62.02A	Hardware and software consultancy
62.02B	Third party maintenance of computer systems and applications
62.03Z	Computer facilities management activities
62.09Z	Other information technology and computer service activities
63.11Z	Data processing, hosting and related activities
63.12Z	Web portals
63.91Z	**News agency activities***
63.99Z	Other information service activities

SECTION K: FINANCIAL AND INSURANCE ACTIVITIES

64.11Z	Central banking
64.19Z	Other monetary intermediation
64.20Z	Activities of holding companies
64.30Z	Trusts, funds and similar financial entities
64.91Z	Financial leasing
64.92Z	Other credit granting
64.99Z	Other financial service activities, except insurance and pension funding
65.11Z	Life insurance
65.12Z	Non-life insurance
65.20Z	Reinsurance
65.30Z	Pension funding
66.11Z	Administration of financial markets
66.12Z	**Security and commodity contracts brokerage***
66.19A	Juridical arrangement of movable property management
66.19B	**Other activities auxiliary to financial services, except insurance and pension funding, ***
66.21Z	**Risk and damage evaluation***
66.22Z	**Activities of insurance agents and brokers***

SECTION K: FINANCIAL AND INSURANCE ACTIVITIES

66.29Z	Other activities auxiliary to insurance and pension funding
66.30Z	Fund management activities

SECTION L: REAL ESTATE ACTIVITIES

68.10Z	**Buying and selling of owned real estate***
68.20A	Letting of dwellings
68.20B	Letting of land and other owned property
68.31Z	**Real estate agencies***
68.32A	**Management of residential building and other real estate on a fee or contractual basis***
68.32B	Juridical arrangement of immovable property management

SECTION M: PROFESSIONAL, SCIENTIFIC AND TECHNICAL ACTIVITIES

69.10Z	**Legal activities***
69.20Z	**Accounting, bookkeeping and auditing activities; tax consultancy***
70.10Z	Activities of head offices
70.21Z	Public relations and communication activities
70.22Z	Business and other management consultancy activities[2]
71.11Z	**Architectural activities***
71.12A	**Surveyor activities***
71.12B	Engineering, technical studies
71.20A	**Car technical testing***
71.20B	**Technical analyses, testing and inspections***
72.11Z	Research and experimental development on biotechnology
72.19Z	Other research and experimental development on natural sciences and engineering
72.20Z	Research and experimental development on social sciences and humanities
73.11Z	Advertising agencies

---

[2] Code used by most *portage* firms

SECTION M: PROFESSIONAL, SCIENTIFIC AND TECHNICAL ACTIVITIES

73.12Z	Media representation
73.20Z	Market research and public opinion polling
74.10Z	Specialised design activities
74.20Z	Photographic activities
74.30Z	Translation and interpretation activities
74.90A	Activities of quantity surveyors
74.90B	**Sundry professional, scientific and technical activities***
75.00Z	**Veterinary activities***

SECTION N: ADMINISTRATIVE AND SUPPORT SERVICE ACTIVITIES

77.11A	Short term renting of cars and light motor vehicles
77.11B	Long term renting of cars and light motor vehicles
77.12Z	Renting and leasing of trucks
77.21Z	Renting and leasing of recreational and sports goods
77.22Z	**Renting of video tapes and disks***
77.29Z	Renting and leasing of other personal and household goods
77.31Z	Renting and leasing of agricultural machinery and equipment
77.32Z	Renting and leasing of construction and civil engineering machinery

	and equipment
77.33Z	Renting and leasing of office machinery and equipment (including computers)
77.34Z	Renting and leasing of water transport equipment
77.35Z	Renting and leasing of air transport equipment
77.39Z	Renting and leasing of other machinery, equipment and tangible goods
77.40Z	Leasing of intellectual property and similar products, except copyrighted works
78.10Z	**Activities of employment placement agencies***
78.20Z	**Temporary employment agency activities***
78.30Z	Other human resources provision
79.11Z	**Travel agency activities***
79.12Z	**Tour operator activities***
79.90Z	**Other reservation service and related activities***
80.10Z	**Private security activities***
80.20Z	**Security systems service activities***
80.30Z	**Investigation activities***
81.10Z	Combined facilities support activities

SECTION N: ADMINISTRATIVE AND SUPPORT SERVICE ACTIVITIES

81.21Z	General cleaning of buildings
81.22Z	**Other building and industrial cleaning activities***
81.29A	Disinfection, insect and rat extermination
81.29B	Other cleaning activities
81.30Z	**Landscape service activities***
82.11Z	**Combined office administrative service activities***
82.19Z	Photocopying, document preparation and other specialised office support activities
82.20Z	Activities of call centres
82.30Z	**Organisation of trade fairs, trade shows and conventions***
82.91Z	**Activities of collection agencies and credit bureaus***
82.92Z	Packaging activities
82.99Z	Other business support service activities

SECTION O: PUBLIC ADMINISTRATION AND DEFENCE; COMPULSORY SOCIAL SECURITY

| 84.11Z | General public administration activities |

| 84.12Z | Regulation of the activities of providing health care, education, cultural services and other social services, excluding social security |

| 84.13Z | Regulation of and contribution to more efficient operation of businesses |

| 84.21Z | Foreign affairs |

| 84.22Z | Defence activities |

| 84.23Z | Justice and judicial activities |

| 84.24Z | Public order and safety activities |

| 84.25Z | Fire service activities |

| 84.30A | Social security general activities |

| 84.30B | Management of supplementary pensions |

| 84.30C | Social distribution of incomes |

SECTION P: EDUCATION

| **85.10Z** | **Pre-school education*** |

| **85.20Z** | **Primary education*** |

| **85.31Z** | **General secondary education*** |

| **85.32Z** | **Technical and vocational secondary education*** |

SECTION P: EDUCATION

85.41Z	**Post-secondary non-tertiary education***
85.42Z	**Tertiary education***
85.51Z	**Sports and recreation education***
85.52Z	**Cultural education***
85.53Z	**Driving school activities***
85.59A	**Continuing education for adults***
85.59B	**Sundry education***
85.60Z	Educational support activities

SECTION Q: HUMAN HEALTH AND SOCIAL WORK ACTIVITIES

86.10Z	Hospital activities
86.21Z	General medical practice activities
86.22A	X-ray diagnosis and radiotherapy activities
86.22B	Surgery activities
86.22C	Other specialist medical practice activities
86.23Z	**Dental practice activities***
86.90A	Ambulances
86.90B	Medical analysis laboratory

SECTION Q: HUMAN HEALTH AND SOCIAL WORK ACTIVITIES

86.90C	Collection centres and organ banks
86.90D	**Activities of nurses and midwives***
86.90E	**Activities of professionals in re-education, prosthesis or health devices and chiropodists***
86.90F	**Human health activities ***
87.10A	Residential nursing care activities for the elderly
87.10B	Residential nursing care activities for disabled children
87.10C	Residential nursing care activities for disabled adults and other residential nursing care
87.20A	Residential care activities for mental retardation and mental health
87.20B	Residential care activities for substance abuse
87.30A	**Residential care activities for the elderly***
87.30B	Residential care activities for the disabled
87.90A	Residential care activities for children with difficulties
87.90B	Residential care activities for adults and families with difficulties and other residential care activities
88.10A	**Home help***
88.10B	Other welcome or guidance without accommodation for disabled adults or the elderly
88.10C	Assistance by work

SECTION Q: HUMAN HEALTH AND SOCIAL WORK ACTIVITIES

88.91A	**Welcome facilities for young children***
88.91B	Welcome or guidance without accommodation for disabled children
88.99A	Other welcome or guidance without accommodation for children and teenagers
88.99B	Social work activities without accommodation

SECTION R: ARTS, ENTERTAINMENT AND RECREATION

90.01Z	**Performing arts***
90.02Z	Support activities to performing arts
90.03A	**Artistic creation related to fine arts***
90.03B	**Other artistic creation***
90.04Z	**Operation of arts facilities***
91.01Z	Library and archives activities
91.02Z	Museums activities
91.03Z	Operation of historical sites and buildings and similar visitor attractions
91.04Z	Botanical and zoological gardens and nature reserves activities
92.00Z	Gambling and betting activities
93.11Z	**Operation of sports facilities***

SECTION R: ARTS, ENTERTAINMENT AND RECREATION

93.12Z	Activities of sport clubs
93.13Z	Fitness facilities
93.19Z	**Other sports activities***
93.21Z	Activities of amusement parks and theme parks
93.29Z	**Other amusement and recreation activities***

SECTION S: OTHER SERVICE ACTIVITIES

94.11Z	Activities of business and employers membership organisations
94.12Z	Activities of professional membership organisations
94.20Z	Activities of trade unions
94.91Z	Activities of religious organisations
94.92Z	Activities of political organisations
94.99Z	Other membership organisations based on voluntary membership
95.11Z	Repair of computers and peripheral equipment
95.12Z	Repair of communication equipment
95.21Z	Repair of consumer electronics
95.22Z	Repair of household appliances and home and garden equipment
95.23Z	Repair of footwear and leather goods

SECTION S: OTHER SERVICE ACTIVITIES

95.24Z	**Repair of furniture and home furnishings***
95.25Z	Repair of watches, clocks and jewellery
95.29Z	Repair of other personal and household goods
96.01A	**Washing and dry cleaning general services***
96.01B	**Washing and dry cleaning household services***
96.02A	**Hairdressing***
96.02B	**Beauty treatment***
96.03Z	**Funeral and related activities***
96.04Z	**Physical well-being activities***
96.09Z	**Other personal service activities ***

SECTION T: OTHER ACTIVITIES

97.00Z	Activities of households as employers of domestic personnel
98.10Z	Undifferentiated goods-producing activities of private households for own use
98.20Z	Undifferentiated service-producing activities of private households for own use

SECTION U: EXTRATERRITORIAL ORGANISATIONS AND BODIES

99.00Z	Activities of extraterritorial organisations and bodies

Appendix B:
Regulated professions and trades

All of the professions listed with an asterisk in the above tables are regulated in some way; either for consumer protection purposes, animal welfare, hygiene, control of hazardous substances or shameless French protectionism! The right-hand column contains notes if proof of capability or qualifications are required before you are allowed to trade on a permanent basis. If you intend to trade under the auto-entrepreneur system however, most of these prerequisites do not apply.

Generally speaking, if you are an EU citizen, you are allowed to undertake any profession you wish, non-EU nationals by contrast face much stiffer rules before they can operate in France. Be aware though, even if you fulfil the conditions of trade for your profession, the regulatory body may reserve the right to reject your application anyway. This may simply be to test your mettle and persistence; so if at first you don't succeed - try, try again. Some trade bodies might require you to take additional training or exams (in French) in order to prove that you know how to adapt your skills to the needs of the French market. Note too, that any profession that requires you to have direct contact with customers will require a good level of proficiency in the French language.

Happily, for many crafts and trades, the authorities will let you practise without needing to be recognised as an approved qualified professional tradesman – provided you only work on an occasional or temporary basis (i.e. not full time) and have some proof of qualification or professional experience. Also, even if you have selected an NAF code that corresponds with one or more of these regulated professions, you may still not be subject to regulations if your business activity does not correspond directly with a regulated trade.

The conditions also assume you will be trading with French clients and residents, which means if you are going to be remote-working exclusively with clients in another country then these rules may make your life unnecessarily difficult. The solution then is to choose a different unregulated profession that in some way encompasses what you do; the authorities are unlikely to question your decision (NAF code) unless you start servicing French customers.

You can find more information on the professions listed below on www.apce.com under *Activités et professions réglementées*. To summarise – in order to make your life easier, it is best to choose a profession not listed here.

Trade or profession	NAF codes	Qualifications
Abattoir	10.11Z, 10.12Z	
Agricultural and rural land consultant		Must possess a relevant degree or other certified qualification and three years professional experience OR seven years professional experience.
Animal grooming	96.09Z	
Animal/pet carer	96.09Z	Must possess certified professional qualifications or experience.
Antiques dealer	47.79Z, 47.99B	
Architect	71.11Z	Must possess a recognised architects qualification, and evidence of at least three years professional experience – both certified by a recognised architects regulator
Art Gallery	47.78C	
Artist		Must be a practising artist, possess a recognised arts qualification and submit a letter of motivation
Artists managing agent	74.90B	

Trade or profession	NAF codes	Qualifications
Auditor	69.20Z	Must possess the relevant French qualifications or experience
Bailiff	69.10Z	Must possess a recognised law qualification – certified by a recognised legal institution.
Baker	10.71C	To apply for a certificate of professional qualification you must possess a French bakers qualification or equivalent French bakery experience OR be in possession of an equivalent bakers qualification and have at least three years professional experience
Beautician	96.02B	To apply for a certificate of professional qualification you must possess a French beauticians qualification or equivalent French experience OR be in possession of an equivalent beauticians qualification and have at least three years professional experience
Bed and Breakfast	55.20Z	
Buildings inspector	71.20B	Minimum five years experience in France.
Bureau de change	66.12Z	Possess at least six months financial / accounting experience or have had formal training

Trade or profession	NAF codes	Qualifications
Butcher	47.22Z, 47.81Z, 10.11Z	To apply for a certificate of professional qualification you must possess a French butchers qualification or equivalent French butchering experience OR be in possession of an equivalent butchers qualification and have at least three years professional experience
Camp site	55.30Z	
Carpenter/Joiner	43.32A, 43.32B	To apply for a certificate of professional qualification you must possess a French carpenters qualification or equivalent French experience OR be in possession of an equivalent carpenters qualification and have at least three years professional experience
Charcutier	47.22Z, 47.81Z, 10.13B	To apply for a certificate of professional qualification you must possess a French charcuterie qualification or equivalent French experience OR be in possession of an equivalent charcuterie qualification and have at least three years professional experience
Chartered Accountant	69.20Z	Must possess relevant qualification and/or at least two years professionally certified experience
Chauffeur driven hire cars	49.32Z	Proof of professional training, qualifications or experience

Trade or profession	NAF codes	Qualifications
Chimney Sweep	81.22Z	To apply for a certificate of professional qualification you must possess a French Chimney sweeping qualification or equivalent French experience OR be in possession of an equivalent Chimney sweeping qualification and have at least three years professional experience
Clock/Watchmaker	26.52Z	May have to take an induction course.
Confectioner	10.82Z, 10.52Z	To apply for a certificate of professional qualification you must possess a French confectionery qualification or equivalent French experience OR be in possession of an equivalent confectionery qualification and have at least three years professional experience
Construction inspector	71.20B	Must possess a recognised professional qualification – certified by a recognised industry regulator.
Construction worker	43.29A, 43.29B, 43.31Z, 43.34Z, 43.32A, 43.32B, 43.33Z, 43.91A, 43.91B, 43.99A, 43.99B, 43.99C, 43.99D	To apply for a certificate of professional qualification you must possess a French building qualification or equivalent French building experience OR be in possession of an equivalent building qualification and have at least three years professional experience

Trade or profession	NAF codes	Qualifications
Cycle/Motorcycle taxis	49.32Z	
Dance instructor	85.52Z	Must possess relevant training, experience and qualification by recognised institution.
Dance school	85.52Z	
Debt collector	82.91Z	
Demolition	43.11Z	
Dental surgeon	86.23Z	Must possess a recognised degree in dental surgery.
Dietician	86.90F	Proof of French language skills required and must possess relevant training, experience or qualification by recognised institution.
Discotheque	93.29Z, 56.30Z	
Domicile-establishing company	82.11Z	
Drinking establishment	56.30Z, 47.99B	
Driving school	85.53Z	
Dyer	96.01B, 96.01A	

Trade or profession	NAF codes	Qualifications
Electrician	43.21A	To apply for a certificate of professional qualification you must possess a French electricians qualification or equivalent French experience OR be in possession of an equivalent electricians qualification and have at least three years professional experience
Employment Agency	78.10Z	
Estate agent	68.31Z	Proof of French language skills required.
Estate/Buildings manager	68.32A	Proof of French language skills required.
Exhibitions organiser	82.30Z	
Exploitation or exploration of the continental shelf	09.90Z, 09.10Z	
Facial Prosthetics	32.50A	Proof of French language skills required and must possess relevant training, experience or qualification by recognised institution.
Farrier	01.62Z	To apply for a certificate of professional qualification you must possess a French farriers qualification or equivalent French experience OR be in possession of an equivalent farriers qualification and have at least three years professional experience

Trade or profession	NAF codes	Qualifications
Fast food takeaway	56.10C	
Financial advisor	66.19B	Must possess relevant French training, qualifications or experience.
Fishmonger	47.23Z	To apply for a certificate of professional qualification you must possess a French fishmongers qualification or equivalent French experience OR be in possession of an equivalent fishmongers qualification and have at least three years professional experience
Floor/carpet layer	43.33Z	To apply for a certificate of professional qualification you must possess a French flooring qualification or equivalent French experience OR be in possession of an equivalent flooring qualification and have at least three years professional experience
Food Ingredient reseller	47.11, 47.21-47.26, 47.29	
Forestry consultant		Must possess a relevant degree or other certified qualification and three years professional experience OR seven years professional experience.

Trade or profession	NAF codes	Qualifications
Freight Carrier	52.29B	Must possess relevant qualification certified by a regulatory body and have at least two years professional experience OR have five years professional experience. Additional training may be required according to the department.
Funeral services	96.03Z	Proof of at least two years professional experience required.
Furniture restorer	95.24Z	
Garden centre / nursery	47.76Z	
Glazier	43.34Z	To apply for a certificate of professional qualification you must possess a French glaziers qualification or equivalent French experience OR be in possession of an equivalent glaziers qualification and have at least three years professional experience
Goldsmith	25.99A, 32.12Z	
Gym	93.11Z	

Trade or profession	NAF codes	Qualifications
Hairdresser (Salon)	96.02A	Proof of French language skills required. Must possess a French hairdressing qualification or equivalent French experience OR have run your own salon for six years OR be in possession of an equivalent hairdressing qualification and have at least three years professional experience
Hairdresser (visiting)	96.02A	To apply for a certificate of professional qualification you must possess a French hairdressing qualification or equivalent French experience OR be in possession of an equivalent hairdressing qualification and have at least three years professional experience
Haulage firm	49.41C	For heavy vehicles (more than 3.5 tonnes) must have passed the relevant exam, have a recognised French qualification or at least 10 years experience. For light vehicles (less than 3.5 tonnes) must have passed the relevant exam or at least 2 years experience.
HGV driver	49.41A, 49.41B, 52.29A	Must possess appropriate license.
High altitude mountain guide	93.19Z	Proof of French language skills required and must possess relevant training, experience or qualification by recognised institution.

Trade or profession	NAF codes	Qualifications
Horse Riding centre	01.43Z, 01.62Z, 85.51Z, 93.19Z	
Hotel	55.10Z	
HVAC technician	43.22B	To apply for a certificate of professional qualification you must possess a French HVAC qualification or equivalent French experience OR be in possession of an equivalent HVAC qualification and have at least three years professional experience
Illustrator or author	90.03B, 90.03A	
Independent Trainer (non sport)	85.59A, 85.59B	
Insurance broker	66.22Z	Must have at least four years of professional experience in France OR a relevant French qualification
Jeweller	47.77Z, 32.12Z, 32.13Z	
Landscaper	81.30Z, 71.11Z	
Lawyer / Barrister	69.10Z	Must possess a recognised law qualification – certified by a recognised legal regulator.
LGV driver	49.41A, 49.41B, 52.29A, 53.20Z	Must possess appropriate license.

Trade or profession	NAF codes	Qualifications
Lifts/elevator inspector	71.20B	Must possess at least five years installation and maintenance experience in France plus three years inspection experience.
Local Radio	60.10Z	
Locksmith	43.32B	To apply for a certificate of professional qualification you must possess a French locksmiths qualification or equivalent French experience OR be in possession of an equivalent locksmiths qualification and have at least three years professional experience
M.O.T. test centre	71.20A	Must have had at least 35 hours training and possess a relevant French motor-mechanics qualification
Market stall holder		
Marriage/dating agent	96.09Z	
Mason	43.99C	To apply for a certificate of professional qualification you must possess a French masons qualification or equivalent French experience OR be in possession of an equivalent masons qualification and have at least three years professional experience

Trade or profession	NAF codes	Qualifications
Medicine home delivery	53.20Z, 49.41B	Must possess the appropriate French qualification or have at least two years professional experience
Midwife	86.90D	Must be a qualified midwife.
Mineral water production	11.07A	
Minicab	49.39B, 49.32Z	
Modelling agency	78.10Z	
Newsagent	46.18Z, 47.62Z, 46.49Z	
Non-consumable Ingredient reseller	47.19, 47.3 – 47.7, 47.82, 47.89, 47.9	
Notary / Solicitor	69.10Z	You must be a French national to qualify.
Nurse	86.90D	Must have proof of nursing qualification and French language skills.
Nursery for under 6 years	88.91A	
Nursing home	87.30A, 87.10A	Must possess necessary French qualifications

Trade or profession	NAF codes	Qualifications
Occupational Therapist	86.90E	Proof of French language skills required and must possess relevant training, experience or qualification by recognised institution.
Ocularist	32.50A	Must have proof of an Ocularist qualification and French language skills.
Optician	47.78A	Proof of French language skills required and must possess relevant training, experience or qualification by recognised institution.
Orthopaedist	32.50A	Proof of French language skills required and must possess relevant training, experience and qualification by recognised institution.
Orthoptist	86.90E	Proof of French language skills required and must possess relevant training, experience and qualification by recognised institution.
Osteopath	86.90E	Proof of French language skills required and must possess relevant training, experience and qualification by recognised institution.

Trade or profession	NAF codes	Qualifications
Painter and decorator	43.34Z	To apply for a certificate of professional qualification you must possess a French painters qualification or equivalent French experience OR be in possession of an equivalent painters qualification and have at least three years professional experience
Panel beater / car-body mechanic	45.20A, 45.20B	To apply for a certificate of professional qualification you must possess a French panel beater qualification or equivalent French experience OR be in possession of an equivalent panel beating qualification and have at least three years professional experience
Pastry chef	10.71C, 10.71D	To apply for a certificate of professional qualification you must possess a French pastry chefs qualification or equivalent French experience OR be in possession of an equivalent pastry chefs qualification and have at least three years professional experience
Pedorthist	32.50A	Proof of French language skills required and must possess relevant training, experience and qualification by recognised institution.
Periodical Press	58.13Z, 58.14Z	
Personal services		

Trade or profession	NAF codes	Qualifications
Pet / domestic animal retailer	47.76Z	Proof of prior animal care and handling skills required.
Pharmacist	47.73Z	Must possess pharmacists training, experience and qualification by recognised institution.
Physiotherapist	86.90E	Must have proof of physiotherapy qualification and French language skills.
Plasterer	43.31Z	To apply for a certificate of professional qualification you must possess a French plasterers qualification or equivalent French experience OR be in possession of an equivalent plasterers qualification and have at least three years professional experience
Plumber	43.22A, 43.22B	To apply for a certificate of professional qualification you must possess a French plumbers qualification or equivalent French experience OR be in possession of an equivalent plumbers qualification and have at least three years professional experience
Podiatrist	86.90E	Proof of French language skills required and must possess relevant training, experience and qualification by recognised institution.
Press agency	63.91Z	

Trade or profession	NAF codes	Qualifications
Private Investigator	80.30Z	
Private school	85.10Z, 85.20Z, 85.31Z, 85.32Z, 85.41Z, 85.42Z	
Private state school	85.10Z, 85.20Z, 85.31Z, 85.32Z, 85.41Z	
Professional training	85.59A	
Property Auctioneer	47.99B	Must possess relevant qualification or experience.
Property speculator	68.10Z	
Prosthetist	32.50A	Proof of French language skills required and must possess relevant training, experience and qualification by recognised institution.
Psychologist	78.10Z, 96.09Z, 86.90F	One or more qualifications permitting Psychology practice certified by a recognise institution or regulatory body.
Psychomotor Therapist	86.90E	Proof of French language skills required and must possess relevant training, experience and qualification by recognised institution.

Trade or profession	NAF codes	Qualifications
Psychotherapist	86.90F	Must have a French medical doctorate or masters and have at least 400 hours training and five months professional experience.
Publisher	58.11Z	
Removals	49.42Z	
Retirement home / Day centre (non medical)	87.30A	Must possess necessary French qualifications
River freight broker	52.29B	Must possess relevant French qualification plus at least three years professional experience
Rural holiday cottage	55.20Z	
Sales agent		
Second-hand dealer	47.79Z	
Secure transport	80.10Z	Proof of professional experience or qualifications required.
Security agent / bodyguard	80.20Z	
Self service launderette	96.01B	
Ski monitor	85.51Z	Must possess relevant training, experience or qualification by recognised institution and have proof or French language skills.

Trade or profession	NAF codes	Qualifications
Speech therapist	86.90E	Proof of French language skills required and must possess relevant training, experience and qualification by recognised institution.
Sports agent	74.90B	At least two years professional experience or a recognised qualification
Sports coach	85.51Z	Proof of French language skills required and must possess relevant training, experience or qualification by recognised institution.
Stone worker	23.70Z	To apply for a certificate of professional qualification you must possess a French stone workers qualification or equivalent French experience OR be in possession of an equivalent stoneworkers qualification and have at least three years professional experience
Surveyor	71.12A	Must possess relevant qualification and experience. May be required to undergo a further three years training before being allowed to trade.
Swimming pool facilities	93.11Z	
Tanning station	96.04Z	

Trade or profession	NAF codes	Qualifications
Tattoos / piercings	96.09Z	Must complete a course in hygiene and cleanliness.
Taxis	49.32Z	Must take an induction course or aptitude test AND have at least two years previous professional experience or a professional qualification
Tea room	56.10C	
Temp Agency	78.20Z	
Terracing	43.12B, 43.12A	
Theatrical producer	90.01Z, 90.04Z	Must have at least one year's professional experience in France OR at least 500 hours training OR a French diploma.
Tile layer	43.33Z	To apply for a certificate of professional qualification you must possess a French tiling qualification or equivalent French tiling experience OR be in possession of an equivalent tiling qualification and have at least three years professional experience
Tobacconist	47.26Z	
Tour guide	79.90Z	Must possess relevant training, experience or qualification according to the activity.

Trade or profession	NAF codes	Qualifications
Traditional Restaurant	56.10A	
Travel Agent	79.11Z, 79.12Z	Proof of at least four months training, one year's professional experience or a related diploma or qualification.
TV surveillance and electronic security	80.20Z	Proof of qualification or professional experience required.
Vehicle damage assessor	66.21Z	Must possess relevant training, experience or qualification by recognised institution.
Vehicle repair and maintenance	45.20A, 45.20B	To apply for a certificate of professional qualification you must possess a French motor mechanics qualification or equivalent French experience OR be in possession of an equivalent motor mechanics qualification and have at least three years professional experience
Vet	75.00Z	Must have proof of veterinary qualification.
Video club	77.22Z	
Wholesaler	46.22Z, 46.3	
Wines and Spirits broker	46.17B	Must possess a certified qualification of wines and spirits broking experience by a recognised institution.

Disclaimer

I have endeavoured to ensure all information in this first issue of *Freelance in France* is up to date and relevant for 2015, however please be aware that during my research I found many official sites that were either offline or more than a year out of date, which unfortunately means that you might find the occasional inaccuracy.

If you should discover any issues I would be very grateful if you would get in touch so that I may correct them for future editions of this book.

You may email me on info@freelanceinfrance.fr or visit www.freelanceinfrance.fr.

Index

194

www.ingramcontent.com/pod-product-compliance
Lightning Source LLC
Chambersburg PA
CBHW060845170526
45158CB00001B/237